11/16/2018

The Believers
Foundation for
Spiritual Maturity

The Believers Foundation for Spiritual Maturity

Layman to Leadership School of Ministry

Bishop O.J. McIntyre

To order additional copies of this book, contact:

O.J. MCINTYRE MINISTRIES
505-325-1094

ojmcintyre@yahoo.com
For booking information, call 5053265619
69637

Dedication

This Book is lovingly dedicated to:
To the Glory and Honor of my lord and savior
Jesus Christ Who is the author and finisher of my faith

Doris

My darling wife for more than three decades whose love, and
Support, for me never failed to keep me focused on the things of the kingdom.

And the loving community of Restoration Family Worship Center
Whose unfailing support and loyalty for their Pastor as we endeavor
To
Take the gospel of Jesus Christ to the Navajo nation.

The first shall be last
And the last shall be first.

Lesson ONE:
THE BIBLE
THE WORD OF GOD

Lesson ONE: THE BIBLE THE WORD OF GOD

I. INTRODUCTION 11

II. WHAT IS THE BIBLE?...11
   A. The Old Testament 11
      1. Original language
      2. Archaeological proofs
      3. How it was recorded
   B. The New Testament..13
      1. Original Language
      2. How it was recorded
      3. How it was compiled
   C. Progressive Revelation 15

III. THE NATURE OF THE WORD 16
   A. Alive and Powerful...16
      1. God's agent
      2. The effects
   B. Eternal 17
      1. Unfailing
      2. Reliable

IV. HOW TO PROFIT FROM THE WORD.............................17
   A. Mix Faith with the Word 18
      1. The evil report
      2. The truth
      3. Faith vs. unbelief
      4. The Word vs. circumstances
   B. Plant the Word as a Seed 19
      1. The first step
      2. Time
      3. Trust & patience
      4. The full harvest

V. HOW TO ESTABLISH THE WORD IN YOUR LIFE 20

  A. Read the Word 20

    1. Set a time

    2. Set a goal

    3. Pray

    4. Make no exceptions

  B. Study the Word 22

    1. Some tools for studying

    2. Some methods of study

  C. Meditate on the Word 24

VI. SUMMARY—GIVE THE WORD FIRST PLACE 24

Lesson ONE: THE BIBLE THE WORD OF GOD

I. INTRODUCTION

A study of the Bible must begin with recognition of its divine authority as the Word of God. The Bible is a record of God's word to man, recorded by men who were moved by the Holy Spirit (II Peter 1:21). Since it is the Word of God and not the word of men, its power and authority originate with God Himself. All scripture is inspired by God ("God-breathed"—II Timothy 3:16) and so has all the integrity and dependability of God.

Any attempt to understand God and His ways without the Word of God is fruitless. The Bible must be the starting point of all doctrinal discussion, because it is God's revelation of Himself to mankind.

II. WHAT IS THE BIBLE?

The Bible is made up of 66 books, divided into two testaments (i.e. covenants): the Old Testament and the New Testament. It was written down by approximately 44 inspired authors over a period spanning 1600 years. The Old Testament contains 39 books, spanning the time period from the creation of the world to the return of the Israelites from Babylonian exile. The New Testament contains 27 books, covering the time from Jesus' birth to the end of the 1 st century. (See the end of this lesson for an overview of all the books of the Bible.)

A. THE OLD TESTAMENT

The 39 books of the Old Testament can be divided into five major parts: Pentateuch, History, Poetry, the Major Prophets, and the Minor Prophets. These books contain the story of God's dealings with His chosen people, the Israelites, and are recognized by Jews today as their canon (the genuine and inspired scriptures, God's Word to the Jewish people). The major divisions of the Old Testament are as follows:

The Law (Pentateuch)—Genesis Exodus Leviticus Numbers Deuteronomy

History—
Joshua Judges Ruth
I & II Samuel
I & II Kings
I & II Chronicles Ezra Nehemiah Esther

Poetry & Wisdom—
Job
Psalms
Proverbs Ecclesiastes Song of Solomon

Major Prophets-
Isaiah Jeremiah Lamentations Ezekiel Daniel
Minor Prophets—
Hosea Joel
Amos Obadiah
Jonah Micah Nahum Habakkuk Zephaniah Haggai Zechariah Malachi

1. Original language

The Old Testament was written down in Hebrew, a Semitic language akin to Arabic. Small segments of Ezra, Daniel, and one verse in Jeremiah, are written in Aramaic (the language of Palestine in Jesus' day).

2. Archaeological proofs

Numerous attempts by critical scholars have failed to prove that facts listed in the Old Testament are erroneous. Here is just one of many examples:

At least 47 times the Old Testament makes mention of a group of people called the "Hittites." However, in no other ancient writings was there any mention of this nation. Skeptical scholars, during the late 19th century, used to point out this "mythical" kingdom as proof that one couldn't trust the historical facts written in the Old Testament. Then, in 1906, a German archaeologist unearthed the ruins of a large city in modern-day Turkey, which proved to be the capital of a vast empire, the Hittite empire. Its existence had up to this time been little known and only suspected by archaeologists, yet the Old Testament had been speaking of Hittites for thousands of years.

Merrill Unger—

Unger's Bible Dictionary

3. How it was recorded

Although at first God's revelations were oral (Genesis 15:1), He later commanded that what He had spoken should be written down (Exodus 34:27). Throughout the history of Israel, there were men who recorded what God was doing or saying (Numbers 33:2; Deuteronomy 17:18; Joshua 24:26; I Samuel 10:25; Isaiah 8:16; Jeremiah 36:2).

These writings were the scriptures to the people of God at that time, and God expected them to revere them as such (Joshua 1:8; Psalm 1:2). These books have been passed down to our day, and make up what is now known as the Old Testament.

When reading the Old Testament, it is important that one realize that all the books in it look forward. When man fell, God promised a redeemer (Genesis 3:15), and the books of the Old Testament point to that Redeemer. Whether by allusion or direct prophecy, you'll find Jesus in every book of the Old Testament.

The Old Testament is the story of the nation Israel, but it is also God's repeated promise that He was going to send a Redeemer to purchase our salvation.

B. THE NEW TESTAMENT

The New Testament consists of 27 books, written by 8 authors over a 50 year period. It can be roughly divided into five segments: the Gospels, History, the Epistles of Paul, the General Epistles, and Revelation.

The Gospels are a record of the life, death and resurrection of Jesus Christ; the Acts give you a history of the early church; the Epistles are letters from apostles to churches, explaining Christian doctrines; Revelation is John's record of a vision of the end times that he received while in exile on the isle of Patmos.

While the Old Testament contains God's promise of a Redeemer, the New Testament tells us how that Redeemer came and what He accomplished. The major divisions of the New Testament are as follows:

Gospels—Matthew Mark Luke John
History—Acts
Epistles of Paul—Romans 1 & II Thessalonians I & II Corinthians I & II Timothy
Galatians Titus
Ephesians Philemon Philippians Colossians
General Epistles—Hebrews
James I & II Peter I, II & III John Jude Prophecy—Revelation

1. Original Language

The New Testament was written in Greek. This includes the gospels, even though the language which Jesus and all the men of Palestine spoke at that time was Aramaic, not Greek.

At the time the New Testament was written, Greek was a world-wide language. A gospel written in Aramaic or Hebrew would only be useful in Palestine, but one written in Greek could be read anywhere in the known world. Thus, the Greek language was an invaluable tool in the early spreading of the gospel.

2. How it was recorded

Although the books of the New Testament are arranged somewhat chronologically, they were not written in that order. The first New Testament "scripture" anyone received in those days was oral, coming from the mouths of those who preached the gospel. Paul commended those who received his teaching "not as the word of men," but as the divinely inspired Word of God (I Thessalonians 2:13),

The first part of the New Testament to be written down was the Epistles (specifically, the Epistles of Paul). These were written during the period 48-60 A.D. The gospels, written from about 60-100 A.D., were recorded from the memory of those who had walked with Jesus while He was on the earth (Luke 1:1, 2).

It is generally believed that the entire New Testament was written before the end of the first century A.D.

3. How it was compiled

It was common practice among the churches in the 1 St century to share and exchange letters written by the apostles to the churches. In fact, this practice was encouraged by Paul himself (Colossians 4:16). In this way, each church began to accumulate the various writings of the apostles. Remember, at this time there were no printing presses; these handwritten copies of the gospels and epistles were the only available scripture. One had to come to the place of fellowship to hear the scriptures; this is why Paul exhorted Timothy to practice the "Public reading of scripture." (I Timothy 4:13).

Consider what those early believers had for New Testament scriptures—a handful of laboriously written copies. What a privilege it is for us to have such easy access to the Word of God. Let's not waste that privilege by failing to read what modern technology has made so conveniently available to us.

C. PROGRESSIVE REVELATION

When studying the Old and New Testaments, the following guideline is an aid in rightly dividing the word of truth: Always interpret the Old Testament in the light of the New Testament! The Bible is progressive revelation. The Old Testament foretells the coming of a Messiah; the gospels tell us of His coming; the Epistles (especially the epistles of Paul) tell what He accomplished through His death and resurrection.

One cannot understand all the things written in the Old Testament without knowledge of the New Testament revelation of Christ. Even the men who wrote the Old Testament under the inspiration of the Holy Spirit didn't fully understand what they had written, because Christ had not yet been revealed (I Peter 1:10,11). The Ethiopian eunuch needed someone with a working knowledge of this New Testament revelation to explain to him the meaning of Isaiah 53 (Acts 8:30-35).

With the New Testament to shed light on it, the Old Testament becomes a rich treasury of the knowledge of God, full of examples and instruction which are invaluable to a New Covenant believer (I Corinthians 10:11).

III. THE NATURE OF THE WORD

Although it is interesting and helpful to study how the books of the Bible were written down and compiled, we must never lose sight of its real nature. The Bible is much more than just a book it is the Word of God, and as such it is supernatural! By His Word God created the world and the universe (Hebrews 11:3), and even to this day ". **All things are upheld by the Word of His power" (Hebrews 1:3).** God's Word is

A. ALIVE AND POWERFUL

God's Word is Far from being a dead book; the Word of God is living and powerful. It has within it all the life and power necessary to maintain a believer in victory. Paul had such confidence in this fact that he could leave the Ephesian church while it was still in its infancy; he was convinced that the Word was able to build them up and sustain them (Acts 20:32).

1. God's agent
God's Word is the agent by which He accomplishes His will on the earth. God created the world by His Word (Genesis 1:3; Psalm 33:6, 9). Men are born again by the Word (I Peter 1:23). God heals by His Word (Psalm 107:20). God's Word is His power.

2. The effects
Because it is alive and powerful, God's Word has a profound effect wherever it is preached. In Acts 19 we find the record of a mighty move of God's Spirit which took place in Ephesus and affected all of Asia Minor (modern-day Turkey). The sick were healed, demons were cast out, and many came out of occult practices to serve the Lord. Acts 19:16-20, gives us a clue as to why all this took place: "So the Word of God was growing mightily and prevailing."

God's Word was the source of all this outpouring, because God's Word is His power. Here we see an example of what Paul meant when he said, "I am not ashamed of the gospel (Word of God) because it is the POWER OF GOD unto salvation to all who believe." (Romans 1:16).

B. ETERNAL

Read I Peter 1:23

Jesus said to His disciples, "Heaven and earth will pass away, but my words shall not pass away" (Matthew 24:35).

God's Word is an eternal, absolute reality that cannot be altered. It is as unchanging as God is unchanging. As far as God is concerned, what He has spoken is " . . . settled forever in Heaven" (Psalm 119:89).

1. Unfailing

One can be assured of the absolute integrity of God's Word; it cannot fail. God Himself stands behind every promise that He has made (Jeremiah 1:12), and has stated that His Word will not return to Him empty, or fruitless (Isaiah 55:10, 11).

2. Reliable

"God is not a man that He should lie, neither the son of man that He should repent; hath He said, and shall He not do it? Or hath He spoken and shall He not make it good?" (Numbers 23:19 KJV).

A person's word is only as reliable as that person's character warrants. The word of a liar or a cheat would not be very valuable; even a good man's word is not absolutely reliable, because that good man could change with time. We have this assurance about God: He does not lie, and He cannot change (Numbers 23:19; James 1:17). God's Word is reliable because God Himself is reliable.

Our assurance and faith lie in the Word of God, a God who cannot lie, and who cannot fail.

IV. HOW TO PROFIT FROM THE WORD

We have seen that the Bible is a supernatural book, and as God's Word, it contains all the power and life necessary to meet any one of our needs.

However, there is a part which we must play in order to appropriate all the power that the Word has for us.

A. MIX FAITH WITH THE WORD

In Hebrews 4:1-3 we are told that although the Word was preached to the children of Israel, it did not profit them, because they didn't mix it with faith.

Read Numbers 13:17-33.

1. The evil report
Here we find the account of the spies going into the land of Canaan and coming back with a report that was directly Opposite to what the Word of God said. The ten spies with the evil report said that they were as grasshoppers in their own sight.

In reality, with God on their side and with His Word promising their victory, they were conquerors; they could not have failed. But, they chose to put their faith in what they saw and so perceived themselves as grasshoppers.

2. The truth
All the power needed for them to take possession of the land was made available when God spoke His Word; yet that power was of no avail to them, because they didn't appropriate it. The problem lay not with God, nor with His Word (the truth), but with the people of God. Their lack of faith kept the Word from prospering them as God had intended.

3. Faith vs. unbelief
Faith is the factor that activates the Word of God and brings out the great power resident in it. The Word won't work for you unless you mix faith with it. This doesn't mean that the Word lacks for power; all scripture is profitable, even if some don't profit through unbelief. Their unbelief doesn't decrease the profitability of God's Word in any way.

4. The Word vs. circumstances
The children of Israel chose to put their faith in the circumstances how thick the walls were, how tall the giants were rather than in God's promise

that He would fight for them. Thus, they failed to appropriate the power and blessings of God.

The lesson we can learn from their mistake is this: Never Base your judgments, with regard to any situation, upon circumstances which you face. Always judge the matter by the Word of God!

B. PLANT THE WORD AS A SEED

In numerous parables in the gospels, Jesus likened the Word of God to a seed (Mark 4:14, 26, 31). The Word is called many things in the scriptures (e.g. a sword, a light, a rock, etc.), but in these parables Jesus is trying to show how the power in God's Word can be released. As a seed have life and power, so God's Word has life and power. If you know how to release the power in a seed, then you'll know how to release the power in the Word.

Seed is of benefit only if it is planted; seed in a seed bag won't grow. The same is true of God's Word; if it's not planted in our hearts, but left sitting on the shelf or even in our minds, it will never produce the harvest which God intended it to. The Word contains all the power that will ever be needed to produce results, but as with seed, if it's left sitting, and not planted, nothing will happen. However, if you treat it like seed, and plant it in your heart, it will work for you.

Read Mark 4:26-28. From this parable, we can see some principles regarding how to receive a harvest from the Word.

1. The first step
The first step in getting God's Word to work for you is to put it in your heart. Find the appropriate scriptures that pertain to what you need from God and plant it in your heart by meditating upon it. Faith is the way to receive from God, and faith won't come until the Word is planted in you.

2. Time
Once the seed is planted, the man in the parable sleeps and rises, that is, goes about his business, and the seed sprouts. We must believe God's Word is working even when we see no results; seed doesn't sprout the instant it is planted. Put the Word in your heart and don't become discouraged if you don't see immediate results.

3. Trust & patience

The seed grows, and the man doesn't know how. It is not necessary for you to understand how God is going to work; just believe the Word and leave it planted. "Trust in the Lord with all your heart, and lean not to your own understanding. In all your ways, acknowledge Him, and He will direct your paths" (Proverbs 3:5-6).

4. The full harvest

The fruit, in this parable, comes forth and matures in stages' First the blade, then the ear then the full corn in the ear. God's Word brings forth the manifestation in stages, so you may not see full deliverance, prosperity, or healing immediately.

Some, when they see improvement, but not total manifestation, become discouraged, and give up. They see a blade, and think that's all they're going to get; or the parable waited and received the blade, then the ear, and finally the full corn in the ear. If you leave the Word planted and don't give up, you'll receive the full harvest that God intends His Word to produce.

V. HOW TO ESTABLISH THE WORD IN YOUR LIFE

We have seen that the Word is the power of God, and how it will prosper anyone who puts faith in it. But, how does a believer establish God's Word in his own life? How can he deepen his knowledge of God and His Word? This doesn't happen accidentally! It only happens when a believer makes a quality decision to come to know the scriptures. Throughout the Bible God speaks of the value of giving careful attention to His Word (Deuteronomy 11:18-31; Joshua 1:8; Psalm 19:7,8; 119:9,11; Proverbs 4:20-22; Acts 17:11).

"Watch over your heart with all diligence, for from it flow the springs of life" (Proverbs 4:23). The key to establishing your heart in the Word is diligence. If a believer will diligently give attention to the scriptures, he'll find his knowledge of God and God's Word growing deeper and deeper.

A. READ THE WORD

Giving careful attention to the Word begins by establishing a daily discipline of Bible reading. Any believer's knowledge of the Word will not start with "heavy-duty" revelations, but with disciplined daily Bible reading. You've got to read it before God can reveal anything to you.

Many Christians get discouraged with daily Bible reading because they don't get revelation every time they read. The fact is, however, that whether you feel like it or not, reading the Word has a very positive effect on your inner man. "The precepts of the Lord are right, rejoicing the heart" (Psalm 19:8).

Jesus said, "Man shall not live on bread alone, but on every word that proceeds out of the mouth of God" (Matthew 4:4), and "the words that I have spoken to you are spirit and life" (John 6:63). The Bible is food for your spirit, and every time you read, your inner man is being fed, even when your emotions don't feel like this is the case.

Here are some suggestions to help you establish a daily Bible reading habit:

1. Set a time
Set apart a time of the day when you can read your Bible. This time should be compatible with your schedule, so that you can keep it consistently.

2. Set a goal
Set a Bible reading goal for yourself. There are many reading schedules available which will enable you to read through the entire Bible in one year.

3. Pray
Pray before you read. "Open my eyes, that I may behold wonderful things from Thy law" (Psalm 119:18). Also read Ephesians 1:17, 18.

4. Make no exceptions
Make no exceptions once you have established your daily reading schedule. Don't allow anything to pre-empt it. Our daily time in the Bible should be as important to us as our daily bread (Matthew 4:4; Psalm 119:103). Some have committed themselves to the following rule: No Bible, no breakfast.

It's obvious that establishing this time of Bible reading will involve some degree of discipline. But lest we think that discipline is "bondage" and "unspiritual," let's read what Paul wrote to Timothy: "Be diligent to present yourself approved to God as a workman who does not need to be ashamed, handling accurately the word of truth" (II Timothy 2:15). Paul also said that we should discipline ourselves for the purpose of godliness (I Timothy 4:7).

B. STUDY THE WORD

Studying the Word involves a little more than just reading. In Acts 17 the Bereans are noted for examining the scriptures daily." (Acts 17:11) in order to understand what Paul was preaching. Sometimes, in order to fully understand a certain doctrine or passage of scripture, one must read the text more than once and compare it with other scriptures on the same subject (i.e. cross—reference). This, of course, demands more time than reading, but the rewards in understanding the scriptures are rich.

1. **Some tools for studying**
a. An accurate Bible translation, one with which you are comfortable and accommodates your vocabulary (e.g. New American Standard, New International, King James, Revised Standard Versions).

b. **Amplified Bible**—A translation of the Bible that expands the meaning of the original languages.

c. **Bible concordance**—A concordance lists alphabetically all the words used in the Bible with Their context and location (be sure that the concordance you buy matches the translation of Bible that you read, e.g. Young's, Strong's, Cruden's).

d. **Bible Dictionary**—Defines Biblical names, places, and concepts (Unger's, Zondervan, Davis).

e. **Bible Handbook**—A synopsis of the entire Bible, giving much historical and geographical background information (Halley, Unger's).
The Vine's Expository Dictionary of New Testament Words

f. **Pen and notebook**—Write down what you discover from your examining of the scriptures. The above listed tools of study are suggestions to help you in your study of the scriptures. They are not requirements for this course; neither are they requirements for a real understanding of the Bible. They are, however, very useful if they are kept in their proper perspective. They are tools for study, not the thing to be studied.

2. Some methods of study

a   Read your entire Bible. Every Christian should read the Bible all the way through. Use a daily Bible reading plan that will systematically take you through the whole Bible in a specified period of time. The plan which we have included at the end of this lesson will take you from Genesis to Revelation in one year at the rate of about 20 minutes of reading per day.

b.   **Bible study by chapters.** Outline chapters according to author, time period, main subject, main thoughts, key verses, and key words.

c.   **Bible study by words.** By tracing certain words, such as love, grace, healing, the tongue, you'll gain greater insight into the nature of God and the nature of the new creation. Use a concordance or the cross-reference in your Bible margin. A reference Bible will give a notation in the margin or by footnote of related scriptures.

d.   **Bible study by topics.** Closely related to word study is a study of basic Bible topics. By choosing fundamental subjects such as prayer, sowing and reaping, faith, healing, freedom from fear, you can group related scriptures for a greater understanding of Bible principles.

e.   **Bible study by Proverbs.** This book is rich in wisdom and basic moral instruction. It can be studied by outlining each chapter or by tracing basic principles: e.g. contrasts—wisdom and folly, good and evil, diligence and sloth; honesty, family life, mercy, love.

f.   **Bible study by prophecy.** It is of great value to trace the fulfillment of Old Testament prophecy, particularly as it relates to Jesus. It can be done easily in a Bible with marginal cross-references.

C. MEDITATE ON THE WORD

God told Joshua: "This book of the law shall not depart from your mouth, but you shall meditate on it day and night, so that you may be careful to do according to all that is written in it; for then you will make your way prosperous, and then you will have success" (Joshua 1:8).

The word meditate means to mutter to oneself, to muse, to ponder, to reflect. In effect, it is saying the Word to your self over and over again. Meditation will unlock the scriptures to your spirit and enable the Holy Spirit to reveal to you the things of God (I Corinthians 2:11, 12).

As we meditate in the Word and allow the Word to "dwell in us richly" (Colossians 3:16), the Holy Spirit will begin to show us the reality of the spiritual realm which the Word describes (I Corinthians 2:9, 10).

VI. SUMMARY—GIVE THE WORD
FIRST PLACE

God Himself has exalted His Word above even His own name (Psalm 138:2). As His children we also need to exalt the Word and make it the priority in our lives. By putting the Word first in your life, you'll experience far more of God's life and blessing. The Word shows clearly who God is and what He has done in us and for us. God's Word is full of His life and power, and if we'll meditate on it, plant it in our hearts, and mix it with active faith, we'll begin to experience that life and power in fuller and fuller measure.

LESSON ONE

DAY ONE

THE BIBLE—THE WORD OF GOD STUDY QUESTIONS

1. Where does the power and authority of the Bible originate? Give scripture to back up your answer.

   _____

   _____

2. How many books are there in the Bible? _____ O.T. _____
   N.T. _____
a. What time period does the O.T. cover? _____
b. What time period does the N.T. cover? _____
c. the O.T. can be divided into five major parts. Name them:

   _____

d. The N.T. can be divided into five segments. Name them: _____

   _____

3. What is the original language of the Old Testament? _____
   of the New Testament?_____

4. To whom or what do the books of the Old Testament point? Why is it important to interpret the Old Testament in the light of the New Testament? Explain your answer.

   _____

   _____

   _____

5. The Bible is readily available to all in this country. Yet, it has not always been so. In the past, before the advent of the printing press, only a few had the privilege of owning a Bible. Even today, in some countries, believers greatly treasure any portion of the scriptures in print that they can obtain (this is especially true in Communist ruled nations). How does this fact affect your thinking about the scriptures? Explain how you view the Bible, and what it means to you to have such easy access to the scriptures.

   _____

   _____

DAY TWO

THE BIBLE—THE WORD OF GOD STUDY QUESTIONS

1. Each of these scriptures reveals to us a characteristic of the Word of God—the Bible. **Briefly,** state what each scripture reveals about God's Word.

   a. Psalm 119:89 _____

   b. Proverbs 4:22 _____

   c. Isaiah 55:10,11 _____

   d. John 6:63 _____

   e. Acts 20:32 _____

   f. I Thessalonians 2:13 _____

   g. II Timothy 3:16,17 _____

   h. Hebrews 1:3 _____

   i. Hebrews 4:12 _____

   j. I Peter 1:23 _____

2. The Word of God is His agent by which He accomplishes His will on the earth. List three specific things which God accomplishes by His Word. Give scriptures to back up your answer.

   a. _____

   b. _____

   c. _____

3. The Word of God is absolutely reliable, and we can put our full confidence in it. Why? (Numbers 23:19; James 1:17)

   _____

   _____

4. What is the connection between a person's word and his character? How does your knowledge of God's character affect the way you view the Bible? (Psalm 119:90)

   _____

   _____

   _____

   _____

   _____

Lesson TWO:
THE NATURE OF GOD

Lesson 2 THE NATURE OF GOD

I. INTRODUCTION 31

II. THE ATTRIBUTES OF GOD...31
    A. Omnipotence...32
    B. Omnipresence...33
    C. Omniscience...33
    D. The trinity...34
        1. Unity within the God-head
        2. Distinction of persons within the God-head

III. THE NATURE OF GOD 36
    A. Man's image of god...37
        1. Sin distorts man's image of God
        2. Satan defames God's character
        3. Religion affects man's thinking
    B. God's image revealed—jesus 39
        I. His teaching/Love
        2. His life/Love personified
    C. Knowing god's love...41
        1. Renewing our minds
        2. Holding fast our confidence
    D. God's true nature..43

IV. SUMMARY—THE ALMIGHTY—OUR LOVING FATHER 43

Lesson 2 THE NATURE OF GOD

I. INTRODUCTION

God's existence and power are clearly seen in the created world in which we live. These things are shown to all men, and can be known by them, apart from any direct revelation by God through His spoken or written Word. The creation points unmistakably to a divine Creator (Romans 1:19, 20) Paul, when preaching to unregenerate pagans, said of God,

"He did not leave Himself without witness, in that He did good and gave you rains from heaven and fruitful seasons, satisfying your hearts with food and gladness" (Acts 14:17).

God has not left man without an indication of His presence Men who deny the existence of God, the Bible labels as "fools" (Psalm 14:1), who suppress the truth which the creation plainly reveals (Romans 1:18). The created world is evidence for God's existence and power which cannot honestly be denied or ignored. Creation points to its own Author, the Almighty God.

However, a deeper understanding of God's nature and character, beyond the fact that He exists and is powerful, can be gained only through the Word of God. Since the beginning of creation, God has communicated with men, progressively revealing more and more about Himself. We have this revelation of God, today, in the scriptures. The Bible is the means by which God brings us to a deeper understanding of Himself and His ways. It is through the scriptures that we come to understand that God is holy and righteous. The Bible reveals God's love to us by showing all that He did for us in Christ. He has not hidden Himself from man. Through His revealed Word, God has openly showed His nature and character.

II. THE ATTRIBUTES OF GOD

When God created man, He created him in His own image and likeness (Genesis 1:26). Thus, in many respects, man is like God; God is a spirit, and He created man a spirit being. He gave to man a free will and a rational mind, which is able to reason. But there are some attributes which belong to God alone, and to no other created being. These are attributes which define God as the Creator, the Almighty One of the Universe. "In the beginning, God created the heavens and the earth" (Genesis 1:1). In the beginning, before anything was, God was there. God existed before anything existed; no one and nothing created Him, because He has always been (Colossians 1:17; Revelation 1:8). God's pre-existence places Him in a position of absolute supremacy. Everything that exists is there because God created it. "Before the mountains were born, or Thou didst give birth to the earth and the world, even from everlasting to everlasting, Thou art God" (Psalm 90:2).

There are many created beings in the universe, and they all bear, to some degree, the imprint of their Maker. But there is only one Creator, and that is God. Thus, the qualities which define God as supreme are those that belong only to Him. God is all-powerful (omnipotent); He is all-knowing (Omniscient); and He is present everywhere at the same time (omnipresent). No man or angel can Claim these attributes, for they are what define God as God. There is only one God and He is supreme over all that He has created.

A. OMNIPOTENCE

God is all-powerful. That is one of His exclusive attributes. The Bible describes God's acts and accomplishments as those which only an omnipotent God could perform. "To whom then will you liken me that I should be his equal?' says the Holy One.' Lift up your eyes on high and see who has created these stars, the One who leads forth their host by number, He calls them all by name; because of the greatness of His might and the strength of His power not one of them is missing' "(Isaiah 40:25, 26). There is no created being, whether human or angelic, which equals God in power and ability. Throughout the scriptures, God is referred to as "Almighty" (Genesis 17:1; Genesis 35:11; Revelation 4:8). God is Almighty because only He is all-powerful.

Because He is omnipotent, there is nothing that is beyond God's ability (Jeremiah 32:17). God's power is sufficient to bring about all His purposes and plans (Isaiah 46:10, 11). All this God can do without in any way diminishing Himself. When He exerts power, or endues one of His creatures with it, His own power is never lessened. "The Everlasting God, the Lord, the Creator of the ends of the earth does not become weary or tired" (Isaiah 40:28). God is all-powerful, and so is able to do whatever He wills. However, God's will is always consistent with His divine nature. He will never use His power to do anything which contradicts that nature. Thus we find that there are certain things that God cannot do. The Bible says that God cannot lie (Titus 1:2), and He cannot deny Himself (II Timothy 2:13). God's supreme power always operates within the confines of His righteous and loving nature God cannot sin, nor can He ignore sin in others, because to do so would be to deny His very nature. Omnipotence does not mean that God uses His power arbitrarily, irrespective of the limits which His character sets. God is not governed by His power; He always governs that power in keeping with His divine character and nature.

B. OMNIPRESENCE

Another one of God's divine attributes is that of omnipresence. Omnipresence means that God is present everywhere at the same time. This does not mean that God and creation are one and the same (Pantheism); God is separate and distinct from His creation. But He is dynamically present everywhere in that creation. 'Am I a God who is near,' says the Lord, 'And not a God far off? Can a man hide himself in hiding places, so I do not see him?' declares the Lord. 'Do I not fill the heavens and the earth?' declares the Lord" (Jeremiah 23:23, 24). God's presence fills the universe that He made. David declared that no matter where he went, the presence of God's Spirit was there with him (Psalm 139:7-12). When Solomon dedicated the Temple, the "house of the Lord," he confessed That God's presence could not be confined to a building (II Chronicles 6:18).

Only God is omnipresent. He shares this attribute with no other created being. No man and no angel is present everywhere at the same time. (This means that Satan, a fallen angel, is not omnipresent. He can only be in one place at any given moment of time.) Because He is omnipresent, nothing escapes God's notice. Even the smallest sparrow does not go unnoticed by God (Luke 12:6). No good thing done goes unnoticed by God, and no sin committed goes unobserved by the all-present One (Psalm 94:7-9).

C. OMNISCIENCE

God's omnipresence point directly to another of His divine attributes that of omniscience. To be omniscient means to be all-knowing. Omniscience is intrinsic to God's very nature. His knowledge is not derived from any source outside of Himself. In other words, nobody "taught" God anything! "Who has directed the Spirit of the Lord or as His counselor has informed Him? With whom did He consult and who gave Him understanding? And who taught Him in the path of justice and taught Him knowledge, and informed Him of the way of understanding?" (Isaiah 40:13, 14) God has always known everything there is to know. He sees and knows all that has happened in the past, all that is now happening, and all that will happen in the future. Only God is omniscient. No man or angel can claim to be all—knowing. God's reprimand of Job is a commentary on the immeasurability of God's Understanding as compared with the finiteness of man's understands (Job 38:4, 18). Only God is Infinite in understanding (Psalm 147:5). Man is finite in his understanding. Any knowledge which a man has was derived from an outside source. But God's knowledge is not externally derived; it is an eternal attribute of His infinite nature. "Great is our Lord, and abundant in strength; His understanding is infinite" (Psalm 147:5).

The Bible says that God knew about us before the foundation of the world, and predestined us to adoption as His very own children (Ephesians 1:3, 4). He knows everything about us, and is familiar with all of our thoughts (Psalm 139:1-3); nothing is hidden from Him. If we live uprightly, we can derive comfort from knowing that God is aware of everything we do and the motivation behind our actions. In fact, God knows us better than we know ourselves. That is why David prayed, "Search me, 0 Lord, and know my heart; try me and know my thoughts; and see if there be any hurtful way in me, and lead me in the everlasting way" (Psalm 139:23,24). And, those who do not live uprightly must not think that their actions go unobserved by the all-knowing, all—seeing God.

D. THE TRINITY

The trinity of the God-head is one of the profound mysteries of Christianity. To understand the Trinity is to understand how God can be one God, and yet three distinct persons simultaneously. A proper perception of the Trinity is essential, as misunderstanding of this truth has, in the past, led To error and heresy within the Church the three distinct persons of the God-head are the Father, the Son (Jesus Christ), and the Holy Spirit. Each of These persons are fully God, none being subordinate to the others. And yet these three persons are one God, not three Gods. The paradox of the Trinity is how there can be unity and plurality in God at the same time. These two concepts must be held in balance in order to retain a correct view of the God-head emphasizing the unity of God, at the expense of the plurality of God, will lead to error. By the same token, emphasizing the plurality of God at the expense of His unity will cause the same problem.

The Trinity of the God-head involves two paradoxical concepts, the unity of God and the distinction of persons within the God-head. We will look at each of these separately.

1. Unity within the God-head
"Hear, O Israel! The Lord our God, the Lord is one!" (Deuteronomy 6:4; Exodus 20:3-7). When God took the children of Israel out of Egypt, He called them away from the polytheism (i.e. worship of many gods) of the surrounding nations, telling them that there is only one God in heaven The God of Abraham, Isaac, and Jacob This theme is reiterated throughout the Old Testament; there are no gods but God alone (Isaiah 43:10; 45:5). God is called the "only true God" (John 17:3), because every idol which people might worship is in reality a "false god" (I Corinthians 8:4), which the scripture labels "lying vanities."

(Read Jeremiah 10:1-16).

2. Distinction of persons within the God-head
The Scriptures clearly teach that there is a plurality within the unified God-head. "Then God said, 'Let Us make man in our image, according to our likeness.' (Genesis 1:26). God is not addressing the angelic host here, for the creation of man is ascribed exclusively to God. The use of the plurals "Us" and "Our" in this verse is a reference to the three Persons of the Trinity. These Persons are distinguished at the baptism of Jesus (Read Luke 3:21, 22). Here we see the Son, being endued with the Holy Spirit, while the Father speaks His approval from heaven.

The three Persons of the Trinity (Father, Son, and Holy Spirit) are indeed Persons, and not merely manifestations or modes of God. Jesus, the Son, was sent by the Father (I John 4:10), and returned to the Father (John 17:13), at whose right hand He is now seated (Mark 16:19). The Spirit who was promised by the Father, was sent by the Son after His ascension

(Acts 2:33). This is one of many examples in which we see the distinction between the Persons of the Trinity (Matthew 28:19; II Corinthians 13:14; John 14:16, 17, 20-23). These scriptures become absurd and meaningless if the Father, Son and Holy Spirit are viewed merely as manifestations of one God. Manifestations don't converse with one another; neither do they express mutual affection for one another (John 12:27, 28; 17:24). These are the actions and activities of persons, not manifestations or modes.

Each of the Persons within the Trinity is fully God. God is not divided. The Bible says of Jesus, "For in Him (Jesus) all the fullness of Deity dwells in bodily form" (Colossians 2:9). Jesus is no less God than the Father Himself (John 1:1). The scriptures also clearly equate the Holy Spirit with God. When Peter rebuked Ananias, for "lying to the Holy Spirit," he said, "You have not lied to men, but to God" (Acts 5:3, 4). The Trinity of the God-head must not be viewed as three Gods. There is only one God. God's being is in three Persons, each one equal to the other, each one fully God, each one possessing all the attributes and characteristics that make God who He is.

III. THE NATURE OF GOD

God's nature is best described by the word Love. Although this isn't the only characteristic of His nature, it supersedes all others and is the one by which all the actions of God recorded in the Bible must be judged. The Bible says that God is Love (I John 4:8, 16). He defines what the word Love means.

As believers, we must keep this revelation of God's character foremost in our thinking. God is Love, and He desires only good for us all the days of our lives. Because of His love, God promised a redeemer on the very day that man fell (Genesis 3:15). Because of His love, He fulfilled that promise by sending His own Son (John 3:16). Because of His love, He redeemed us through Christ and seated us with Himself in heavenly places (Ephesians 2:4-6).

Our perception of God's character must be rooted in a revelation of the love of God. Unless a person sees clearly how much God loves him, his concept of God will be twisted and marred by fear. God's intentions toward him will never be clear in his own thinking.

A. MAN'S IMAGE OF GOD

To clearly understand God's love for us, we must begin by erasing from our minds some common misunderstandings about God's character. These misconceptions are prevalent among unbelievers, and a surprising number of Christians. They are rooted in the fall and used by Satan to paint a dark and twisted picture of God in men's minds.

1. Sin distorts man's image of God

God created man to have fellowship with Him. Sin not only destroyed that fellowship, but also distorted man's image of God. Because of sin, man lost sight of the fact that God is a loving Father.

The fear that entered into him because of sin, (Genesis 3:10) kept man from being able to see God as He really is, Sin put God far away from man; He was now a Being that struck terror in the minds of those to whom He appeared. Recall the Israelites' reaction to the manifestation of God's presence (Exodus 19:18, 19). They told Moses to talk to God for them; they would stay in the background—at a safe distance.

Using man's distorted conception of God to his advantage, the enemy seeks to this day to deceive men about God's true character and intentions. In II Corinthians 4:4, Paul says the following concerning unbelievers: "in whose case, the god of this world has blinded the minds of the unbelieving that they might not see the light of the gospel of the glory of Christ, who is the image of God." The god of this world is Satan. He is the one who is trying to convince unbelievers that God doesn't love them. He is the one who blinds their minds to the gospel, a gospel which boldly proclaims to all men that God loves them, that He has reconciled Himself to them through His Son; God is entreating them even now, "Be reconciled to Me!" (II Corinthians 5:19, 20). Satan must keep unbelievers ignorant of this gospel revelation, for if they understood it, there would be no question as to whom they would serve.

Not only has Satan deceived and blinded unbelievers, but he has also deceived many believers. He comes to them with the commonly accepted lie that God is a withholder. The Bible clearly states that God is a liberal giver (James 1:5), and that He will not withhold any good thing from those who Walk uprightly (Psalm 84:11). Read Genesis 3:1-5. In this account of Satan's temptation of Eve, the tempter told Eve that the real reason God didn't want them to eat from the tree of knowledge was because He was holding out on them. Satan planted in Eve's mind the idea that God's intentions toward her did not altogether love and that God was withholding good things from her.

Believers must settle in their own hearts and minds that God loves them, and is not holding out on them. The fact that God sent His own Son to die for us is eternal, unfading proof that He is a liberal giver and not a withholder (Ephesians 1:7; Romans 5:8). "He who did not spare His own Son, but delivered Him up for us all, how will He not with Him freely give us all things?" (Romans 8:32).

3. Religion affects man's thinking

Religion (by which we mean a set of ideas about God formed largely by the traditions of men, rather than the Word of God) has done much to promote an incorrect image of God in men's minds. Traditions of men have portrayed God as being an angry ogre, ready to strike down any offender. He is never thought of as loving, only stern and austere. This type of thinking was prevalent in Jesus' day, even among His own disciples. Read Luke 9:52-56. James and John (called the "Sons of Thunder" by Jesus in Mark 3:17) were ready to call fire down from heaven. They assumed that God's reaction to the Samaritan rejection of Christ would be the same as theirs. Jesus' response to them shows that they did not in any way understand the heart of the Father God, nor His reason for sending the Son. James and John projected onto God their own ways of thinking and responding to people.

Many Christians make the same mistake with regard to God's love toward them. They assume that God's ways and thoughts are just like man's ways and thoughts; they project their own carnal thinking about themselves onto God. Many times they base their concept of God's ways upon what they would do if they were God, just as James and John did. But, God says, "For My thoughts are not your thoughts, neither are your ways my ways. For As the heavens are higher than the earth, so are my ways higher than your ways, and My thoughts than your thoughts" (Isaiah 55:8, 9). Never assume that you know what God is thinking unless He tells you through His Word. Presumption always leads to misunderstanding.

B. GOD'S IMAGE REVEALED—JESUS

As we have already seen, man's concept of God is blackened by sin and twisted by religious tradition. But, God has a way to show man what He is really like, to reveal His true nature. That way is Jesus.

In Hebrews 1:3, Jesus is called "the radiance of His (God's) glory, the exact representation of His nature." Jesus exactly represents God and His great love for man. He is, in effect, God's statement to the world: "Here is what I am like! This is how much I love you!"

In every way Jesus exemplifies the love of God, not only in the fact that He was sent by God (John 3:16), and that He died for our sins (Romans 5:8), but also in the manner in which He conducted His ministry while here on the earth. The teaching and lifestyle of Jesus during His earth walk reveal a God with a heart full of compassion and love.

I. His teaching/Love

Whenever Jesus instructed His disciples, He always referred to God as "Father" and "your Father." The Jews knew God as "Yaweh," a name considered so holy that they were not allowed to say it audibly. Jesus came calling Yaweh, "Daddy" (Matthew 6:4, 8, 9).

He knew that God was by nature a Father and that before the foundation of the world, God had wanted a family (Ephesians 1:4, 5). So He introduced Yaweh to the world as a "heavenly Father," One that is infinitely good and infinitely loving.

In Matthew 7:7-11, Jesus was teaching His disciples that God would answer their prayers and that the reason He would do so was because He is a loving Father. He said that no normal father would give his child stones and snakes when asked for bread and fish; in other words, no father gives evil, harmful things to his children. He would be considered warped and sadistic if he did so. The Father God is far better than any "evil," earthly Father. "If you then, being evil, know how to give good gifts to your children, HOW MUCH MORE shall your Father who is in heaven give what is good to those who ask Him!" (Matthew 7:11). God doesn't give "stones" and "snakes" to His children; if a believer is getting "stones" and "snakes" in his life, he can be sure that they are not coming from the Father in heaven.

"In that day you will ask (the Father) in my name, and I do not say to you that I will request the Father on your behalf, for the Father Himself loves you . . ."(John 16:26, 27). Jesus is saying that He won't have to ask the Father for us; God will answer because He loves us. Jesus prayed, at the end of His time on earth that " . . . the world may know that Thou didst send me, and didst love them even as Thou didst love me" (John 17:23). No one has any difficulty believing that God loves Jesus; Jesus is His only begotten Son. God would do anything for Jesus But; here we are told that God loves us just as much as He loves Jesus. This is in keeping with the fact that God loved man so much, that He considered it worth the price of His own Son to redeem him from the hand of sin and Satan.

2. His life/Love personified

Not only did Jesus' teachings reflect the love of God, but His earthly life did as well. We see the compassion of God flowing from Jesus toward the lost, the hungry, the maimed, and the sick. He " . . . went about doing good, and healing all who were oppressed by the devil, for God was with Him" (Acts 10:38). When Jesus was moved with compassion, and healed the sick (Matthew 14:14), it was because God the Father wanted the sick healed. When Jesus was moved with compassion and fed the multitude (Matthew 15:32-37), it was because God the Father wanted the people fed. When Jesus was moved with compassion and told the disciples to pray the Lord to send laborers forth (Matthew 9:36-38), it was because God the Father wanted the lost multitudes saved. Jesus was moved with compassion because God was moved with compassion.

Jesus showed us beyond any doubt that God is a loving Father. His words and deeds were witnesses to this fact. Jesus didn't come representing an angry ogre, ready to condemn and destroy. Jesus came showing us a Father that wanted to reconcile to Himself the creature that He loved, a Father who wanted to save lost man from sin and death.

"For God sent not His Son into the world to condemn the world; but that the world through Him might be saved". (John 3:17 KJV)

C. KNOWING GOD'S LOVE

The Church needs a revelation of the Love of God. We need to see it so clearly that our first thoughts at the start of the day are of God's love for us. Ignorance of the fact that God loves them has left many Christians spiritually paralyzed, unable to move with any boldness in the things of God. God has " . . . granted unto us everything pertaining to life and godliness, through the true knowledge of Him . . ."(II Peter 1:3). We will not be able to fully appropriate all the things that God has given to us, unless we come to a full knowledge of who God is; we must know that He perfectly defines the word Love.

1. Renewing our minds

Paul prayed for the Ephesian church, a church noted for its maturity in the Lord, that they "being rooted and grounded in love, may be able to comprehend with all the saints what is the breadth, and length and height and depth, and to know the love of Christ which surpasses knowledge, that you may be filled up to all the fullness of God" (Ephesians 3:17-19). Paul was praying that they receive a supernatural revelation of God's love. It is only by a revelation of the Holy Spirit that we can "know" something which "surpasses knowledge." Only by the Spirit of God will our minds be able to grasp the immensity of God's love.

Because God's love goes beyond human reasoning, your intellect and emotions can't always be trusted to comprehend the love of God. Unfortunately, many believers base their assurance of God's love on their feelings, or on what they can figure out with their minds. They get up in the morning and see what state their emotions are in to determine whether God still loves them or not.

Your emotions can't tell you anything about the love of God. When a person has to experience a certain emotion before he'll believe that God really loves him, it's the same as asking God for a "sign" that His Word is true. God has given us all the proof we'll ever need to show us how great His love is. He sent His only begotten Son into the world to die, and watched Him hang on a cross, just so He could redeem us to Himself.

Knowledge of God's love comes through meditating on the new covenant revelation of what He has done for us, and why He has done it. "But God, being rich in mercy, because of His great love with which He loved us, even when we were dead in our transgressions, made us alive together with Christ (by grace you have been saved), and raised us up with Him, and seated us with Him in the heavenly places, in Christ Jesus, in order that in the ages to come He might show the surpassing riches of His grace in kindness toward us in Christ Jesus" (Ephesians 2:4-7).

"And do not be conformed to this world, but be transformed by the renewing of your mind . . ." (Romans 12:2) we must have our minds renewed to the fact that God loves us. To wallow around in feelings of insecurity, inadequacy, and inferiority is nothing more than being conformed to this world. The world is trapped with these kinds of emotions because they have a twisted picture of God, but through His Word, God has revealed to us His true nature. He has shown us that He is a loving Father! As we renew our minds, the love of God will become a concrete reality for us knowing that God is for us and not against us will be so integrated into our thought patterns that the mere suggestion of inadequacy or insecurity will seem absurd **"If God be for us, who can be against us?"** (Romans 8:31).

2. Holding fast our confidence
In Hebrews we are told that in order to please God we must believe something specific about His character; we must believe that He is a rewarder (Hebrews 11:6). Confidence in God is not possible unless a person believes that He is a rewarder and a liberal giver (James 1:7).

The apostle John said, "And we have come to know and to believe the love which God has for us "(I John 4:16). Again, we find the principle of believing something about God's character; not only did John know about the love of God, but he also believed it. John had received a revelation of God; God is love! "There is no fear in love; but perfect love casts out fear . . ."(I John 4:18). John knew that being free from fear, and having confidence before God were results of knowing and believing the love of God. When one has such a deep-rooted revelation of God's love that he can say "God is Love," being afraid of God is out of the question; confidence before Him becomes very natural.

No one will begin to experience this freedom from fear and confidence before God until he puts faith in the fact that God loves him. In Hebrews 11:1, faith is called an assurance. In Hebrews 3:14 we are told to "hold fast the beginning of our assurance firm until the end." You have to hold firmly to the assurance of God's love. It is impossible to believe that God is a rewarder and a withholder at the same time; the two are incompatible. Either He is a rewarder, or He is a withholder; He can't be both. But, the Bible is explicit as to the true character of God. God is a rewarder (Hebrews 11:6); He is a liberal giver (James 1:5); He will not withhold any good thing from those who walk uprightly (Psalm 84:11).

D. GOD'S TRUE NATURE

God's nature is Love; it always has been, and it always will be. The world, through sin and the deceits of Satan has developed a wrong picture of God. It has viewed God as angry and demanding, a person to be greatly feared. But, when God sent His only Son Jesus, He presented to the world the most profound evidence of love divinely possible. Through Jesus, God showed man once and for all the true nature of His character.

For too long the Church has been paralyzed by an unnecessary fear of God. She has lacked the Fill confidence to move boldly in the areas where God has needed her. But, the Church today is awakening to the fact that God will not hold out on them it was this confidence that enabled the early church to do the mighty works which it did. They had a revelation of God's love for them; they knew He would answer their prayers and requests, because He loved them. As today's church begins to get "rooted and grounded in love," (the revelation of God's love), she will begin to move in the boldness required to do the works of Jesus and the greater works that He referred to in John 14:12.

IV. SUMMARY—THE ALMIGHTY—OUR LOVING FATHER

It is essential for a proper perspective of God, to understand His position of supremacy. Everything that exists is there because God created it. In His position of supremacy, God has attributes which cannot be shared by any other creature. These are the attributes which define God as God. God is all powerful; there is nothing that can diminish His might. God is all knowing; there is nothing that He does not know. God is present everywhere at the same time; He sees all that occurs anywhere, at any given moment of time. But as vast and powerful as God is, He has not separated Himself from us, or made Himself unapproachable. Knowledge of God's vastness must be tempered with the revelation that "God is love!" All of God's attributes are manifested in keeping with His loving character. Because God is love, He didn't use His power and wisdom against us, but for us. He sent His only Son to purchase our redemption. Thus, God's vast power and knowledge is channeled toward our good and benefit because God is a loving Father. We serve a God who is Almighty and who has no peer. But that Almighty God is a loving Father, whose good intentions are directed toward us, His children.

LESSON TWO
DAY ONE
THE NATURE OF GOD STUDY QUESTIONS

1. Find four scriptures (Old or New Testament) which reveal the pre-existence of God.

    a. _____

    b. _____

    c. _____

    d. _____

2. God's exclusive attributes (i.e. those that belong only to Him) are omnipotence, omniscience, and omnipresence. Briefly define each, and then show how they are displayed in and through God. (Use scripture to support your answer.)

    _____

    _____

    _____

3. List two things which God cannot do—and the scriptures which reveal these things.

    a. _____

    b. _____

4. God's omnipotence, omniscience, and omnipresence are more than mere theological concepts. They are spiritual realities. What do these mean to you? How do they affect your life?

    _____

    _____

    _____

    _____

    _____

LESSON TWO
DAY TWO
THE NATURE OF GOD STUDY QUESTIONS

1. What are the two paradoxical (i.e. seemingly contradictory) concepts involved in the Trinity?

a. _____

b. _____

2. How would you respond to a person who said, "I believe that the Trinity is three separate and distinct gods"? What scriptures would you show that person?

_____

_____

_____

3. Briefly explain the distinction of Persons within the God-head. How is this different from the idea that the Trinity is three manifestations or modes of God?

_____

_____

_____

_____

4. List two scriptures which point to the unity of the God-head.

a. _____

b. _____

List three scriptures which point to the plurality within the God-head.

c. _____

d. _____

e. _____

LESSON TWO
DAY THREE
THE NATURE OF GOD STUDY QUESTIONS

1. What three things have caused man to have a dark and distorted image of God?

   a. _____

   b. _____

   c. _____

   _____

2. Briefly, what is religion?

   _____

   _____

   _____

3. How has a revelation of God's love affected your life? How will it affect you in the future?

   _____

   _____

   _____

4. How does faith relate to our knowledge of God's love?

   _____

   _____

   _____

   _____

5. In order to please God, what must we believe about His character?

   _____

   _____

   _____

   _____

LESSON TWO
DAY THREE
THE NATURE OF GOD STUDY QUESTIONS

1. Jesus reveals God the Father to us, both through His words and His deeds. List the qualities and characteristics of God the Father which are revealed to us in Christ. Then explain how Jesus reveals those qualities. Give specific examples from the words of Jesus and from the actions of Jesus as recorded for us in the Gospels.

_____

_____

_____

_____

_____

_____

_____

_____

_____

_____

2. How would you respond to a believer who said, "God has forsaken me. I just don't feel His love anymore! I feel like God must hate me "? What scriptures would you share with this person, and how would you explain them, in the light of his "feelings"?

_____

_____

_____

_____

_____

_____

_____

_____

_____

Lesson THREE RIGHTEOUSNESS: THE GIFT OF GOD

Lesson three RIGHTEOUSNESS: THE GIFT OF GOD

1. INTRODUCTION 53

II. MAN'S GREAT NEED 53
   A. Man before the fall..54
      1. Created in God's image
      2. God's under-ruler
      3. Freedom of choice
   B. Man After The Fall 55
      1. Spiritual death
      2. The inheritance
   C. Man's Inability to Help Himself...........................56

III. GOD'S ANSWER TO MAN'S NEED 56
   A. Jesus, God's Solution 56
      1. Did the Old Covenant fail?
      2. Atonement under the Old Covenant
   B. Old Testament Figures Pointing to Jesus 57
      1. The blood
      2. The scapegoat
   C. New Testament Fulfillment of Old Testament Figures.............58
      1. The shedding of blood
      2. The identification with sin
   D. The Blood Of Jesus Cleansed Sin 58
      1. The blood of Jesus speaks for us
      2. The blood of Jesus is our receipt
   E. Christ's Identification with Man............................59
      1. Represented in His death
      2. Represented in His resurrection
   F. How God Could Be Just in Justifying.....................60
      1. An acceptable sacrifice
      2. A Son of Adam obedient to death
      3. Divinity
      4. Fully God/fully man

IV. THE FREE GIFT OF RIGHTEOUSNESS 62
   A. Not By Works 63
      1. The Law
      2. Self-righteousness
   B. Righteousness by Faith 64
      1. Our believing
      2. God's grace
      3. Our receiving
   C. How To Avoid the Galatian Error 65
      1. Continuing in grace
      2. Receiving forgiveness

V. THE FFFECT OF RIGHTEOUSNESS 66
   A. Peace with God 67
      1. Jesus removed the sin barrier
      2. Free access to God's presence
   B. Quietness and Confidence 68

VI. ESTABLISHING THE REALITY OF RIGHTEOUSNESS 68
   A. Don't Look to Your Emotions 69
   B. See Yourself As God Sees You 69

VII. SUMMARY—THE VALUE OF RIGHTEOUSNESS 70

Lesson three. RIGHTEOUSNESS: THE GIFT OF GOD

1. INTRODUCTION

E. W. Kenyon defines righteousness as "the ability to stand in the presence of the Father God without the sense of guilt or inferiority." A righteous person is one who has right—standing with God. Without righteousness, fellowship with God is impossible. Adam was created with this kind of right—standing. After he disobeyed, he cowered in the presence of God because of the sin that was then in him (Genesis 3:10). He was no longer in right-standing with God, so fellowship was destroyed.

Before fellowship with God could be re-established, this sin had to be replaced with righteousness. That is what the story of God's redemption is all about: God removed from man the sin which separated him from God and replaced it with His very own righteousness. How God accomplished this and that He was just in doing so, is revealed in the "gospel" (good news) message of the New Testament. For many years the gospel has been preached as a revelation of sin. Preachers have spent great amounts of time telling of the evil which is in mankind. However, in his letter to the Romans, Paul shows us that rather than the gospel being a revelation of sin, it is a revelation of righteousness. He explains how God made His righteousness available to man through faith in .Jesus Christ (Romans 1:16, 17).

Believers need to deepen their understanding of this revelation. God has imparted unto them His own righteousness, and they are therefore in right-standing with Him. God's desire is that we know this so well that we can " . . . draw near with confidence to the throne of grace" (Hebrews 4:16), the very presence of God, free from the fear that Adam experienced after he sinned.

II. MAN'S GREAT NEED

When studying God's redemption of man, it is vital that we understand what it is that we were redeemed from! Paul told the Ephesians that before they were saved, they were by nature the children of wrath (Ephesians 2:3); he said that they were without hope and without God in the world (Ephesians 2:12). Man was under the dominion of darkness and needed to be delivered (Colossians 1:13). As we shall see, only God could accomplish this deliverance.

A. MAN BEFORE THE FALL

When God created Adam, He created him without sin and without flaw, in His own image (Genesis 1:27), and breathed into him His own Spirit (Genesis 2:7). Adam was a perfect creation (Genesis 1:31), able to stand in God's presence without guilt or fear and enjoy fellowship with Him.

1. Created in God's image

Adam was made in the image of God, which set him apart from all the other creatures God had created. He was in God's image in that he was created a spiritual being (Genesis 1:27). God is a Spirit and can only have fellowship with a creature of like kind. So, He made man "a little lower" than Himself, a spirit being with whom He could fellowship.

2. God's under-ruler

Adam was a creature of authority, for God gave him dominion over all the works of His hands (Genesis 1:26, 28). We have little appreciated the extent of his dominion. David said:

Yet Thou hast made him a little lower than God,

And dost crown him with glory and majesty! Thou dost make him to rule over the works of Thy hands; Thou hast put all things under his feet. Psalm 8:5, 6.

Adam was God's under-ruler on the earth, and it was his responsibility to take care of it.

3. Freedom of choice

Adam was also given freedom of choice. It was his prerogative to choose to obey God or to disobey Him. The forbidden tree was placed in the garden (Genesis 2:9) to insure that Adam had this freedom. Without it he would have been little more than a robot, obeying God simply because he had no other option.

The New Testament reveals that before the foundations of the world, God had wanted a family (Ephesians 1:4, 5), which is why He called us into fellowship with Himself and His Son (I Corinthians 1:9; I John 1:3). So He created a being like Himself (in His image), giving him dominion and freedom of choice. With such a creation, He could have fellowship.

B. MAN AFTER THE FALL

God told Adam that if he disobeyed and ate of the forbidden tree, he would die the very day he did so (Genesis 2:17). Simple reading of the Bible text will show that God was not referring to mere physical death, for Adam continued to live physically after his disobedience. The immediate effect of this first sin was inward. The outward manifestation of the inward effect did not occur until nine hundred and thirty years later (Genesis 5:5).

1. Spiritual death

The death to which God referred was spiritual death. The entrance of sin into Adam's life brought separation from God, the source of all life; "for the wages of sin is death" (Romans 6:23). The effect of this corruption of Adam's nature is immediately apparent; Adam tried to hide himself from the presence of God (Genesis 3:8). The unrighteousness which came into Adam as a result of his disobedience made it impossible for him to come freely into God's presence.

2. The inheritance

The effects of Adam's disobedience go far beyond the life of Adam and Eve. We are told in the New Testament that because of Adam, we all died spiritually. For "as in Adam all die, so also in Christ all shall be made alive" (I Corinthians 15:22). Through one man's sin, death (i.e. spiritual death) entered the world and passed upon all men (Romans 5:12). All men have inherited spiritual death from Adam, because they are born with Adam's likeness and image (i.e. his fallen nature) as was Seth (Genesis 5:3).

Thus, the curse of sin passed onto the entire human race as a result of Adam's transgression. David was so aware of this curse that he stated in his prayer of repentance: "Behold, I was brought forth in iniquity, and in sin my mother conceived me" (Psalm 51:5).

C. MAN'S INABILITY TO HELP HIMSELF

Not only did spiritual death pass upon all men, but man was also left powerless to overcome this inward condition. The creature which God had created to rule became a slave to sin, unable to break free and get back into fellowship with God. No amount of good works could ever re-establish the right—standing that Adam had with God before the fall. Man was now by nature an unrighteous creature.

"For all have sinned, and fall short of the glory of God . . ." (Romans 3:23). Paul says that there is none righteous, not one (Romans 3:10). Those who wish to establish their own righteousness by good works are destined to fail and might well cry out as did Paul before his conversion: "Wretched man that I am! Who will set me free from the body of this death?" (Romans 7:24).

III. GOD'S ANSWER TO MAN'S NEED

God didn't cease to love man when he fell and was lost in unrighteousness. If that were the case, no way of salvation would ever have been made by God. God's love for man was too great for Him to let man go to destruction without making a way of deliverance available.

While we were still helpless, at the right time Christ died for the ungodly (Romans 5:6). Man was helpless to regain that position of right-standing with God that Adam had originally enjoyed. God Himself would have to do it for man.

A. JESUS, GOD'S SOLUTION

God's redemption of man revolves around the person of His Son, Jesus. Jesus was God's plan for our redemption from the very beginning. He is the promised redeemer who was to bruise (crush) the serpent's head (Genesis 3:15). On the day that man fell, God had no other redeemer in mind but Jesus. This is why Jesus is called "the Lamb that was slain from the creation of the world" (Revelation 13:8 NIV).

1. Did the Old Covenant fail?

Some are of the mistaken impression that the Old Covenant is a plan of redemption which God tried, but which didn't work. Jesus is understood to be an alternate plan which God enacted after the failure of the first.

But, the Old Covenant was never intended to be the means by which God would free man from the slavery of sin and unrighteousness.

The scriptures are clear on this point. "For it is impossible for the blood of bulls and goats to take away sins" (Hebrews 10:4). "For the Law (i.e. the Old Covenant) can never by the same sacrifices which they offer continually, make perfect those who draw near" (Hebrews 10:1). God never intended the rituals and regulations of the Old Covenant to be the means of man's redemption.

2. Atonement under the Old Covenant

Atonement in the Old Covenant was on the basis of Jesus' sacrifice, since all the animal sacrifices of that covenant look forward to Jesus' death. It was on this basis that God overlooked the transgressions committed under the first covenant (Romans 3:25; Hebrews 9:15).

B. OLD TESTAMENT FIGURES POINTING TO JESUS

As we have already seen, the scriptures of the Old Testament point to Jesus. God instituted animal sacrifice for the forgiveness of sins in order to symbolize that Jesus would come and sacrifice Himself for our sins; " . . . without the shedding of blood there is no forgiveness" (Hebrews 9:22).

The most significant day for the expiation of sin in the Jewish calendar was the Day of Atonement (Yom Kippur). This was the day on which the High Priest made sacrifice for the sins of the people.

Read Leviticus 16:1-28

The sin offering mentioned in this passage is symbolic of the Lord Jesus. Notice that it involved not one, but two goats.

1. The blood

The first goat was to be killed and its blood sprinkled on the mercy seat for the expiation of sin (Leviticus 16:15). Shed blood meant that something had died (Leviticus 17:11). God thus used this blood as a visual reminder to the Jews that their sin had resulted in death (Leviticus 1:5, 11; 3:2, 8; 4:5-7; 5:9).

2. The scapegoat

The second goat was presented to Aaron alive. Laying his hands upon its head, Aaron confessed over it all the sins of the people. Thus, the second goat became the sin-bearer for the people. "And the goat (i.e. the scapegoat) shall bear on itself all their iniquities to a solitary land" (Leviticus 16:21, 22).

C. NEW TESTAMENT FULFILLMENT OF OLD TESTAMENT FIGURES

The rituals described in Leviticus 16 are of course symbolic of Christ's sacrifice. Just as there were two animals for the sin offering, so redemption through Christ is two-fold.

1. The shedding of blood

Jesus shed His blood for the forgiveness and cleansing of our sins. "In Him we have redemption through His blood, the forgiveness of our trespasses, according to the riches of His grace" (Ephesians 1:7).

2. The identification with sin

Jesus was identified with our sins, bearing them and their Penalty. So that we wouldn't have to "He (God) made Him (Jesus) who knew no sin to be sin on our behalf that we might become the righteousness of God in Him" (II Corinthians 5:21).

D. THE BLOOD OF JESUS CLEANSED SIN

Even before His death, Jesus made it plain that remission of sins would only be accomplished with the shedding of His own blood (Mark 14:24). His blood was the price that was paid to redeem us to God (I Peter 1:18, 19).Jesus' blood did something which the blood of animals could never do. The blood of animal sacrifices had only temporary and external effects (Hebrews 9:9, 10; Hebrews 10:1-3). But, the blood of Jesus has a permanent and inward effect (Hebrews 9:12, 14). It is His blood that washed us clean from our sins (Revelation 1:5), making us holy and blameless before the Father.

1. The blood of Jesus speaks for us

The blood of Jesus speaks and avails for us today. In Hebrews 12:24, we are told that we have come to " . . . the sprinkled blood (i.e. Jesus' blood), which speaks better things than the blood of Abel." When Abel was murdered by his brother Cain, God told Cain that Abel's blood was crying out to Him from the ground (Genesis 4:10).

Abel's blood speaks condemnation, but Jesus' blood speaks forgiveness and redemption. Jesus' blood is speaking forgiveness for you at this very moment, telling God that the price for your sin has been paid!

2. The blood of Jesus is our receipt

Jesus shed blood signifies that He poured out His life for us (Leviticus 17:11). The penalty for sin is death, and somebody had to pay that price, either we or somebody else in our behalf. .Jesus paid that price for us, and His blood is our receipt that that debt has been paid.

E. CHRIST'S IDENTIFICATION WITH MAN

Jesus was identified with the sin of mankind, becoming the sin-bearer for humanity. Although He was without sin, God imputed all our sin to Him (i.e. charged it to His account). And Jesus suffered the penalty for it (II Corinthians 5:21). .Just as the scapegoat bore the sin of the Israelites, and was driven into the wilderness, so Jesus bore our sin and was separated from the presence of God (Mark 15:34; Acts 2:27; Romans 10:7).

Jesus didn't just bear the penalty for sin—He bore the sin itself. "But the Lord has caused the iniquity of us all to fall on Him" (Isaiah 53:6, 12). He died 'under the judgment of God and went to the place of departed spirits, called Hades (Acts 2:27) or the abyss (Romans 10:7), where He was separated from God (Mark 15:34). Thus, Jesus' suffering was much more than just physical.

1. Represented in His death

When Jesus died on the cross, everything that had ever alienated us from God died with Him. The sin which had lodged in our spirits and separated us from God was dealt a death blow on the cross. " . . . Our old self (man) was crucified with Him, that our body of sin might be done away with" (Romans 6:6) the "old man" to which Paul refers was our old, spiritually dead nature. Paul was so acutely aware that he was represented in Christ's death that he could say," I have been crucified with Christ" (Galatians 2:20), by which he meant, "The sinful nature (old man) that separated me from God died when Jesus died!"

2. Represented in His resurrection

Not only were we represented in Christ's death, but we were also represented in His resurrection. God "made us alive together with Christ (by grace you have been saved), and raised us up with Him, and seated us with Him in heavenly places, in Christ Jesus" (Ephesians 2:5, 6).

The purpose in Christ's becoming sin for us was that we might be made the righteousness of God. Jesus was imputed with our sin, so that we could be imputed with His righteousness.

F. HOW GOD COULD BE JUST IN JUSTIFYING

When God redeemed man, He had to do so in such a way as was consistent with His character. For God to have simply "let us off the hook" and overlooked our sin would have compromised His righteous nature, making Him a party to Adam's sin. God is holy and just, and as such, He must inflict righteous punishment on all sin. Thus, the wrath of God was justly directed toward man, because by nature man was a sinful creature (Romans 3:23).

But, the Bible says that God sent Jesus to be the propitiation for our sins (Romans 3:25; I John 2:2; 4:10). Propitiation means appeasement or satisfaction. By the sacrifice of Jesus, the just wrath of God was appeased. The wrath that should rightly have fallen on us was focused on Christ as He hung on the cross.

1. An acceptable sacrifice

To be an acceptable sacrifice, Jesus had to be a man without sin. If He had sinned at any point during His life, His death would have been for His sins and not for ours. Before Jesus could be deemed a spotless sacrifice, He had to be tempted in all points like us, and yet not sin. This is why Jesus had to be a man.

If God had just appeared on the scene (an eternal spirit) and not become a man, He would not have been vulnerable to temptation; for "God cannot be tempted by evil" (James 1:13). Only a man can be tempted; so Jesus became a man.

The Bible affirms that Jesus was tempted in every way, yet He never succumbed. (Hebrews 4:15); He always obeyed God. In fact, He lived His entire life in accordance with the precepts of the Mosaic Law. Thus, when He was led away to Calvary, He was indeed a "lamb unblemished and spotless" (I Peter 1:19).

2. A Son of Adam obedient to death

Jesus always referred to Himself as "the Son of Man" (Matthew 11:19; 16:13); He was not an ethereal spirit that floated around the earth for thirty-three years. He was a flesh-and blood human being. "What was from the beginning, what we have heard, what we have seen with our eyes, what we Beheld and our hands handled, Concerning the Word of Life (I John 1:1).

Jesus is called the "last Adam" (1Corinthians 15:45; Romans 5:14, because He came to undo what the first Adam had done. The first Adam fell because he disobeyed God. The Last Adam (Jesus) Obedience to God in the Garden of Gethsemane undid what Adam's disobedience had done in the Garden of Eden.

3. Divinity

However, in order for Jesus to qualify to bear the sins of the whole world and for His sacrifice to be sufficient for all men's sin's He had to be God, Only God could bear on Himself the sins of the whole world (1 John 2:2) only God's life was worth enough to buy back the entire human race.

And thus, we see Jesus continually affirming His divinity. "I and the Father are one" (John 10:30). "Truly, truly, I say to you, before Abraham was born, I am" (John 8:58). In this latter scripture, Jesus used the same expression to describe Himself which God spoke to Moses: "I am that I am" (Exodus 3:14).

4. Fully God/fully man

To be a spotless representative of mankind (Who lived without sin) and to be worthy enough to pay the price for all of man's sins, our Redeemer had to be man and God at the same time. This is exactly what Jesus was. He was fully man in one being.

How could a person be man and God accomplished this through the virgin birth. Jesus was born when the Holy Ghost overshadowed a virgin by the name of Mary and caused her to conceive (Luke 1:35). This was a supernatural occurrence. Jesus was born of a woman (Galatians 4:4). But He was conceived by the Spirit of Almighty God (Matthew1:18-20)! Thus, simultaneously He was fully man and fully God In one being.

And without controversy, great is the Mystery of godliness: God was manifested in the flesh, justified in the Spirit, seen of angels, preached unto the Gentiles, believed on in the world, received Life into glory" (I Timothy 3:16 KJV).

The wages of our sin was death, but God deemed the death of His spotless Son Jesus as sufficient to pay the sin-debt that we all owed. As we have seen, Jesus was a worthy substitute for us, and so God could be " . . . just and the justifier of the one who has faith in Jesus" (Romans 3:26). Our sins weren't overlooked by God. He paid for them Himself at the price of His very own Son.

IV. THE FREE GIFT OF RIGHTEOUSNESS

As we have said, God's motivation for making His own righteousness available was His great Love. God was not obligated in any way to redeem man from the mess that he was in. Man was responsible for the fall, not God. God would have been perfectly justified in letting mankind bear all the punishment for his iniquity.

That God didn't let man go to destruction, but made a way of salvation for him at the price of His own Son, is a testimony to His Grace and Everlasting Mercy (Ephesians 2:7). God has not dealt with us according to our sins, but instead He dealt with His Son according to our sins, thereby making available to us the free gift of righteousness. God saw that man was helpless to reestablish right-standing with Him, so He re-established it for us.

A. NOT BY WORKS

Paul told Titus that we are saved by the mercy of God, and not by our works of righteousness (Titus 3:5). For many, this is a hard fact to accept. **There is nothing any man can ever do that will make him worthy by his own merit to be in right-standing with God.** This is the very truth which the Jews could not comprehend. The Bible says the Jews did not achieve right-standing " . . . because they did not pursue it by faith, but as though it were by works. They stumbled over the stumbling stone (i.e. Jesus)" (Romans 9:32). Righteousness can only be achieved through faith in Jesus Christ; good works will never make anyone righteous.

1. The Law
The Law (by which we mean the commandments of Moses) was never meant to be the way for man to receive righteousness, because " . . . by the works of the Law, no flesh will be justified in His sight; for through the Law comes the knowledge of sin" (Romans 3:20).

The Law was given to show man that he is lost in sin (See Romans 7:14-24 in which Paul describes his state before he was saved), and that he is utterly helpless to achieve right—standing with God on his own merit. Paul called the Law a tutor that brings us to Christ (Galatians 3:24), so that we can be made right by putting our faith in Jesus' sacrifice.

2. Self-righteousness
God's righteousness is a free gift that cannot be earned. If you had to work for it, it wouldn't be a free gift (Romans 4:4, 5). Any righteousness which is based upon works is not God's righteousness but is rather self-righteousness, a righteousness based on the flesh rather than on Jesus' sacrifice.

B. RIGHTEOUSNESS BY FAITH

"For we maintain that a man is justified by faith apart from the works of the Law" (Romans 3:28). Paul is emphatic in his assertion that only faith in Jesus brings about righteousness. If works were capable of making a man righteous, then Christ's suffering and death were a waste of time (Galatians 2:21).

The only way to get a free gift is simply to receive it, and God's method of receiving from Him is Faith (Hebrews 11:6). The only way any man will ever receive the righteousness which God has made available is to receive it by faith!

1. Our believing

"And Abraham believed God, and it was reckoned to him a righteousness" (Romans 4:3). Abraham wasn't justified because he was a good man or because he deserved to be justified. He was justified because he believed we can stand before God without condemnation, not because we worked ourselves to a position of worthiness before Him, but because we have faith in the fact that Jesus' sacrifice was sufficient to eliminate sin. When God sees a man or woman not striving to establish his or her own righteousness, but simply accepting God's free gift and believing in Jesus' all-sufficient sacrifice, God credits them with His very own, holy and pure Righteousness.

2. God's grace

"Therefore it is of faith, that it might be by grace" (Romans 4:16). The fact that God's righteousness can only be received by faith insures that that righteousness is imputed completely on the basis of God's unmerited favor and has nothing to do with our deeds. We are made righteous through faith only because faith is the hand which reaches up and receives the provision of God's Grace (unmerited favor). "For by grace you have been saved, through faith" (Ephesians 2:8).

Faith is not a work to which a Christian can point and then say to God, "See there! I deserve to be justified." A child who receives a gift from his parents doesn't then go out and start bragging about how wonderful he is for the way in which he received the gift. He tells others how wonderful and loving his parents are! In the same way, faith brings glory not to the one who believes, but to the One who bestows the gracious gift which faith receives. "Let him who boasts, boast in the Lord" (I Corinthians 1:31).

3. Our receiving

Faith which receives Christ is as simple an act as when your child receives an apple from you, because you hold it out and promise to give him the apple if he comes for it. The belief and the receiving relate only to an apple; but they make up precisely the same act as the faith which deals with eternal salvation. What the child's hand is to the apple that your faith is to the perfect salvation of Christ. The child's hand does not make the apple, nor improve the apple, nor deserve the apple; it only takes it. And faith is chosen by God to be the receiver of salvation because it does not pretend to create salvation, or to help in it, but it is content humbly to receive it.

Charles Spurgeon—All of Grace

C. HOW TO AVOID THE GALATIAN ERROR

In his letter to the Romans, Paul says that the righteousness of God is "from faith to faith" (Romans 1:17). This means that not only is our right-standing with God established through faith, but it is also continually maintained through faith! Many Christians have the mistaken idea that once you get saved, you then have to maintain your stand with God by doing good works.

This error was prevalent in the Galatian church, and it was the sole reason that Paul wrote a letter to them. That he felt very strongly about this issue can be seen in the way in which he addressed them: "You foolish (i.e. stupid) Galatians! Who as bewitched you . . . ?" (Galatians 3:1). Careful reading of the book of Galatians will reveal that Paul speaks more sternly to this church than he does even to the Corinthian church (which was noted for its carnality and immorality). Paul knew that this error struck at the very heart of Christianity, so he dealt with it sternly.

"Having begun by the Spirit, are you now being perfected by the flesh?" (Galatians 3:3). The Galatians were deceived into thinking that in order to maintain their stand with God, they would have to keep the precepts and commandments of the Mosaic Law (i.e. do good works). Paul calls this kind of teaching "another gospel," which is totally contrary to the one that he preached. He goes on to' say that anyone who preaches such a message should be accursed! (Galatians 1:8).

1. Continuing in grace

Our continuing relationship with God is based upon the same grace that brought us into salvation. We were saved by grace and now we stand, in that same unmerited favor! Through Jesus we have obtained our introduction by faith into this grace in which we stand" (Romans 5:2). You are no more righteous and acceptable in God's sight today than you were on the day in which you were saved. You didn't deserve the favor of God then, and you don't deserve it now! God's favor can never be earned by man. Your right—standing with God is based on the fact that you believe in the sufficiency of Jesus' sacrifice.

2. Receiving forgiveness

If, after we are saved, we succumb to the flesh and stumble in some kind of sin, our forgiveness is based upon the same principles as was our salvation: confession and faith. "If we confess our sins, He is faithful and righteous to forgive us our sins and to cleanse us from all unrighteousness" (I John 1:9).

God forgives us when we stumble on the same basis as He redeemed us—Grace! The idea of penance (doing good deeds to pay for sins) came into being because men thought that they could earn God's forgiveness. Penance is nothing more than the flesh saying, "I don't need the grace of God; I can earn His forgiveness! But, the Bible says, "No flesh should glory in His presence" (I Corinthians 1:29 KJV)

V. THE FFFECT OF RIGHTEOUSNESS

"The work of righteousness will be **peace** and the service of righteousness, quietness and confidence forever" (Isaiah 32:17). When God gave His righteousness to us, He restored us to the right-standing which Adam had enjoyed before the fall. That right-standing has a profound effect upon a person.

- Righteousness returns to him the dominion which God had given Adam at the outset

- Righteousness restores to him the freedom from fear which Adam lost after he fell (Genesis 3:10).

- Righteousness enables him to come into God' presence without any feeling of guilt, inferiority or condemnation.

A. PEACE WITH GOD

"Therefore having been justified by faith, we have peace with God through our Lord Jesus Christ" (Romans 5:1). With the sin that had separated us from God taken out of the way, a relationship without fear can be established between us and God. This is the fellowship which God had desired when He created Adam and to which He predestined us in Love before the foundation of the world (Ephesians 1:4, 5).

1. Jesus removed the sin barrier
There is no longer any barrier between God and us. In fact, we are encouraged to come boldly into the holy place, that is, into the very presence of God (Hebrews 4:16; 10:19 KJV). Under the Old Covenant, the presence of God was a fearsome thing, and the High Priest entered the holy place once a year, and then only after elaborate preparations (Leviticus 16:33, 34).

But, we are under a better covenant than they were, because' Jesus has opened the way into the presence of God for us. We can come freely without any fear (Hebrews 10:19, 20).

2. Free access to God's presence
The exhortation of the scriptures to us is to come freely into God's presence. "Let us draw near with a sincere heart in full assurance of faith" (Hebrews 10:22). God is not pleased when those whom He has redeemed, justified, and sanctified by the Blood of His Son stay away from Him because of fear. He is calling us to "draw near," because He sees us as Holy and blameless (Ephesians 1:4).

We are righteous before God, and so He is at peace with us. The sin and condemnation that caused Adam to fear have been removed (Romans 8:1), so there is no reason for us to be afraid of God. God has imparted to us His own righteousness, the same right-standing that Jesus had when

He walked the earth. "He (God) made Him (Jesus) who knew no sin to be sin on our behalf, that we might become the righteousness of God in Him" (II Corinthians 5:21).

B. QUIETNESS AND CONFIDENCE

There is an assurance and a boldness that comes when a person knows that he is in right-standing with the God who created the universe. The scripture says that "the righteous are bold as a lion" (Proverbs 28:1).

The people of Jesus' day often marveled at the authority and boldness in which Jesus spoke and acted (Mark 1:22, 27). When He prayed before the tomb of Lazarus, He said: "Father, I thank Thee that Thou heardest Me. And I knew that Thou hearest me always" (John 11:41, 42). Jesus was always confident that He had God's ear. That confidence stemmed from His awareness that He was in right-standing with a God Who loved Him and who would do anything that He asked.

When you are in right-standing with God and can stand blameless before Him, that means God is for you, He is on your side! Your quiet assurance comes from this realization: "If God be for us, who can be against us?" (Romans 8:31 KJV), this is the boldness that enabled Peter to tell the cripple at the Beautiful Gate to rise and walk (Acts 3:6). This is the confidence that is able to tell a dead woman to arise (Acts 9:40).

VI. ESTABLISHING THE REALITY OF RIGHTEOUSNESS

Many Christians go through life ignorant of the fact that they have been made the righteousness of God in Christ. They don't know that they have right-standing with God, so they have little confidence to come before Him. The author of Hebrews called this kind of Christian a "babe." "For everyone who partakes only of milk is not accustomed to the word of righteousness, for he is a babe" (Hebrews 5:13)

That these believers don't know that God has made them righteous doesn't in any way negate the truth of that fact. They are righteous whether they know it or not. The sad result, however, is that these people can't avail themselves of all the blessings which right-standing brings. There is no barrier of sin between them and God, but they are convinced that one exists.

Many times this kind of thinking is the result of the gospel being preached as a revelation of sin, rather than a revelation of God's righteousness.

Believers need to establish firmly in their hearts and minds that God has declared them righteous on the basis of Jesus' sacrifice. God sees us as holy and blameless, washed pure from our sins by the blood of His Son. As we affirm in our minds that we are righteous before Him, we will become mature adults, not only "accustomed," but **well-versed in the word of righteousness."**

A. DON'T LOOK TO YOUR EMOTIONS

Emotional feelings can't always be trusted to tell you the truth, so it is foolish to base your assurance of righteousness on emotions. Emotions can change from one day to the next, but your righteousness is based upon the sacrifice of Jesus, and the effects of that sacrifice are eternal and unchanging. No matter what you may feel like, God sees you as holy and blameless, because of Jesus.

Righteousness is by faith (Romans 1:16, 17), and faith is not an emotion. Our right-standing before God is based upon our faith in the work of the cross. When we choose to believe feelings of unworthiness, we are in effect saying that Christ's sacrifice was not sufficient. Put your faith in what the Word says Jesus accomplished for us on Calvary, and not in what your emotions say about your worthiness.

B. SEE YOURSELF AS GOD SEES YOU

The Word of God is the only true reflection of who you are before God. The Word gives us "God's eye view" on reality and tells exactly what God thinks of those whom Christ has redeemed with His blood. As we dwell on what the Word says about us and our place in Christ, our thoughts about ourselves begin to conform to God's thoughts about us.

- The Word says you are the righteousness of God (II Corinthians 5:21), because that is how God sees you!

- The Word says you are holy and blameless before Him (Ephesians 1:4), because that is what God thinks of you

- The Word says you are part of a chosen race, a royal priesthood, a holy nation, a people for God's own possession (I Peter 2:9), because that is how God feels about you! Agree with God and His Word, rather than your emotions. You are a righteous person!

VII. SUMMARY—THE VALUE OF RIGHTEOUSNESS

The value of anything can only be judged by the price that was paid to obtain it. When we see the great price that was paid to forgive us and to impart to us God's righteousness, we can then fully appreciate the value of that righteousness. Our right-standing with God is not lacking in any point, for He has " . . . forgiven us all our transgressions" (Colossians 2:13). There is nothing that can bar us from the presence of God.

"Since therefore, brethren, we have confidence to enter the holy place by the blood of Jesus . . . let us draw near with a sincere heart in full assurance of faith, having our hearts sprinkled clean from an evil conscience and our bodies washed with pure water" (Hebrews 10:19,22).

LESSON THREE

DAY ONE

RIGHTEOUSNESS—THE GIFT OF GOD STUDY QUESTIONS

1. What is the Gospel a revelation of? What does it show us?

   _____

   _____

   _____

   _____

2. Describe man before the fall by listing three different characteristics and/or possessions of Adam, the first man, before he sinned.

   a. _____

   b. _____

   c. _____

3. Adam's sin had a great effect on him as well as on the rest of mankind. How did the fall affect Adam and how does it affect us today (i.e. before we are born again)?

   _____

   _____

   _____

   _____

4. What was God's plan for redemption from the very beginning? Give two scriptures which show that God had no other plan in mind.

   _____

   _____

   _____

   _____

   _____

   _____

LESSON THREE

DAY TWO

RIGHTEOUSNESS—THE GIFT OF GOD STUDY QUESTIONS

a _____

b _____

1. The New Testament states explicitly that the blood of bulls and goats cannot take away sin. Why was God able to forgive (pass over) men's sins on the basis of animal sacrifice under the Old Covenant? Give scripture to support your answer.

   _____

   _____

   _____

   _____

2. The description of the Day of Atonement and the sacrifice of the two goats described in Leviticus 16 symbolize the two-fold nature of Jesus' sacrifice. What were these two basic aspects of Christ's death?

a _____

b _____

3. What is the effect of the blood of Jesus within us? How is Jesus' blood different from the blood of Abel?

   _____

   _____

   _____

4. What does propitiation mean? What does it signify to you?

   _____

   _____

   _____

   _____

LESSON THREE

DAY THREE

RIGHTEOUSNESS—THE GIFT OF GOD STUDY QUESTIONS

1. Briefly explain how each of the following scriptures attests to Jesus' humanity.

   a. Luke 2:7

   _____

   _____

   b. Hebrews 4:15

   _____

   _____

   c. 1 John 1:1

   _____

   _____

2. Why was it necessary for our Redeemer to be fully God and fully man?

   _____

   _____

   _____

3. Fill in the blanks: We were saved by, _____ through _____. Explain why faith is not a work, by which we merit the salvation of God.

   _____

4. How would you respond to a person who said, "I know I'm going to heaven because I Obey all the rules of my church!"? What scriptures would you show him?

   _____

   _____

LESSON THREE

RIGHTEOUSNESS—THE GIFT OF GOD STUDY QUESTIONS
DAY FOUR

1. What was the Galatian error? What was their mistake in understanding?

   _____

   _____

   _____

   How would you share with a person who was caught in this type of thinking?

   _____

   _____

   _____

2. According to Isaiah 32:17, what are the three main effects or works of righteousness in the hearts and minds of believers?

   a. _____

   b. _____

   c. _____

3. How has a revelation of righteousness through Christ changed the way in which you approach God? How has it changed the way you view yourself?

   _____

   _____

   _____

   _____

Lesson FOUR THE NEW CREATION: BORN OF GOD

Lesson FOUR THE NEW CREATION: BORN OF GOD

I. INTRODUCTION 79

II. THE NEW BIRTH 79
   A. Born of the Flesh...80
      1. The father of sin
      2. in Adam vs. in Christ
      3. The condition of the heart
   B. Born of the Spirit...81
      1. Hearts of stone and flesh
      2. Instant and complete transformation
      3. Incorruptible and imperishable seed
   C. Born Into God's Family...82
      1. Born in His likeness—Love
      2. We are children of God

III. RECEIVING ETERNAL LIFE 83
   A. What Is Eternal Life? 84
      1. Eternal life vs. "endless existence"
      2. When eternal life begins
   B. Why Jesus Came 85

IV. NEW CREATURES IN CHRIST 85
   A. New Creation = New Nature...86
      1. Created in His image
      2. Complete re-creation
   B. The Dual-Nature Fallacy 87
      1. Paul's "wretched state"
      2. The reborn man's freedom from sin
   C. Instant Maturity? 88
      I. The need to conform
      2. The need to control

V. GOD'S INDWELLING PRESENCE..89
   A. God's Spirit in the Old Testament...............................89
      1. Where God's anointing was
      2. Where God's presence was
   B. The Promise of God 90
   C. God's Spirit in the New Testament..............................91

VI. SUMMARY—THE SUPERNATURAL, RADICAL, NEW
BIRTH..92

Lesson FOUR THE NEW CREATION: BORN OF GOD

I. INTRODUCTION

Jesus came to relate man, who was lost in sin, back to the Father God. He did this by shedding His own blood for our forgiveness and justification, thus making it possible for us to be born into God's family. "But as many as received Him, to them He gave the right to become children of God, even to those who believe on His name, who were born not of blood, nor of the will of the flesh, nor of the will of man, but (born) of God" (John 1:12,13).

Any man who believes on the Lord Jesus Christ as his Savior is a reborn man, born again out of death into life. The result of the new birth is a miraculous new creation, a creature made in the very image of God in holiness, purity, and love.

This is the purpose behind the new birth: to take a sinful, "old creature," alienated to God, and to recreate him into a righteous, "new creature," alive to God and able to serve God out of his heart, as Adam did before he fell.

II. THE NEW BIRTH

Jesus said to Nicodemus, "You must be born again" (John 3:7). This wasn't given as an option—it was a requirement. When Jesus said this, He wasn't referring to a physical occurrence, as Nicodemus thought (John 3:4). He was speaking of a spiritual occurrence, which would get men into the Kingdom of God. Nicodemus was an aged and respected ruler of the Jews, and yet this position was of no avail to him spiritually. In God's eyes, it makes no difference how important a person is or what a person owns, he has the same need as Nicodemus—He must be born again!

In John chapter 3, Jesus spoke of two births. One makes all men carnal and lost in sin, while the other makes men alive to God. "That which is born of the flesh is flesh and that which is born of the Spirit is spirit" (John 3:6).

A. BORN OF THE FLESH

Every person alive has been born of the flesh, and so has been ushered into the Adamic race by virtue of his physical birth. As such, each person is born in Adam's likeness and image (Genesis 5:3). This is the first birth to which Jesus refers when He says, "You must be born again." This physical birth places all men "in Adam," and thus under the curse of spiritual death (I Corinthians 15:22). Because of this corrupted inward condition, all men must be born again before they can enter God's kingdom.

1. The father of sin

The sinful nature which is in men who are not born again is in reality the nature of the devil. " . . . the devil has sinned from the beginning" (I John 3:8). Jesus told the Pharisees, "You are of your father the devil, and you want to do the desires of your father. He was a murderer from the beginning, and does not stand in the truth, because there is no truth in him ", (John 8:44). The apostle John calls those who don't obey God "children of the devil" (I John 3:10).

2. in Adam vs. in Christ

When Adam sinned, he ceased to be a child of God (as he was created to be) and became a child of the devil because of the sinful nature which came into him. This inward condition was passed on to all of Adam's descendants (except Jesus), so that all men Are born under the authority of darkness—Satan's dominion. There is no neutrality with God; one is either a child of God or a child of the devil—there is no middle ground! If any man is in Adam and not in Christ, then he is still an old creature, ruled and dominated by an inner nature under Satan's dominion.

3. The condition of the heart

Man's inward condition cannot be changed by any amount of good works or acts of righteousness. The Jews of Jesus' day were under the delusion that their acts of piety and rituals of washings kept them spiritually pure. Jesus said that what comes out of a man's heart (i.e. his innermost being) is what defiles him (Mark 7:20-23).

No matter how much you may polish up a rotten apple and make it look good on the outside, it is still rotten on the inside. This is how God views men who are not born again, but who try to do good works (Matthew

23:27). The inner wickedness is the result of a physical birth into the Adamic race (first birth); acts of righteousness won't change that condition any more than polishing the outside of a rotten apple will make the inside of the apple fresh and new.

B. BORN OF THE SPIRIT

When a man is born of the Spirit, it is his second birth (rebirth). Rebirth is simply the removal of the old, corrupted nature and its replacement with a New nature (Colossians 3:9, 10) anyone who has been born of the Spirit (i.e. born again) has "passed out of death into life" (John 5:24); he has been delivered from the authority of darkness and translated into the kingdom of God's Son (the Kingdom of God) (Colossians 1:13, Acts 26:18).

Rebirth does for man what all the false religions of the world can never do. These religions give numerous pious rules for conduct, but they can do nothing about a man's inward condition (Colossians 2:23). It is this inward condition that keeps men out of God's kingdom (Ephesians 2:3). Men are lost today not because of what they do, but Because of what they are! (What they do is a result of what they are).

1. Hearts of stone and flesh
God promised the transformation of the new birth in the Old Testament. "Moreover, I will give you a new heart and put a new spirit within you; and I will remove the heart of stone from your flesh and give you a heart of flesh" (Ezekiel 36:26). The "heart of stone" is the old nature; the new heart ("heart of flesh") and the new spirit are the new nature which comes into a man when he is born again.

Israel habitually sinned and went away from God because they had hearts of stone (Jeremiah 5:23; 7:24). God knew that the only thing that would change their conduct would be to change their hearts (Ezekiel 11:19, 20). This inward change is what occurs at the new birth. Instead of a stony heart which fights God, we have been given a new heart and spirit which are alive to God and desire to do His will.

2. Instant and complete transformation
Being born again is not a gradual process by which we work up to a certain level of development. The new birth is an instantaneous work of

the Holy Spirit that occurs the moment we believe. As we have said, there is no middle ground with God. You are either "in death" or "in life"; you are either a child of the devil or a child of God. There is no such thing as a child of the devil developing into a child of God. You are either one or the other you can't be halfway in between. That **INNER** transformation is complete the moment that you believe. The moment you are born again, you are perfectly delivered from Satan's authority, completely translated into God's kingdom, fully a child of God (Colossians 2:9, 10).

3. Incorruptible and imperishable seed

Not only is the work which the Holy Spirit accomplishes at the new birth instantaneous, but its results are eternal. "For you have been born again not of seed which is perishable, but imperishable, that is, through the living and abiding word of God" (I Peter 1:23). We were brought forth (i.e. born again) by the Word of Truth (James 1:18), and that Word of God abides forever (I Peter 1:24, 25). The new heart which comes into the one who is born again is incorruptible and imperishable because the seed that brought that new heart forth is the Word of God. That which is born of the flesh (Of perishable seed) will fade and pass away (I Peter 1:24), but that which is born of the Spirit (by imperishable seed) will never pass away, but will abide forever (II Corinthians 4:16).

God, before the foundations of the world, had wanted a family, children who would love and serve Him out of a sincere heart. This is why He created Adam; Adam before the fall was a child of God. But when Adam fell, spiritual death passed on all men, and man could no longer be a child of God, because he was no longer like God in his heart.

But when a man is born again, his stony heart is replaced with a new heart. This new heart, which is a result of the working of God's Spirit, is in the likeness of God and "Has been created in righteousness and holiness of the truth" (Ephesians 4:24).

1. Born in His likeness—Love

One can see from simple observation that children bear the physical and emotional characteristics of their parents. The same is true of those who have been born of God. The children of God bear the characteristics of their Father in Heaven, because their inner natures are like God.

God's supreme attribute is Love. The Bible says, "God is Love" (I John 4:16). This is also the main spiritual attribute of His children. "Beloved, let us love one another, for love is from God; and everyone who loves is born of God and knows God. The one who does not love does not know God, for God is Love" (I John 4:7, 8).

Loving one another is not what causes a person to be born again; believing on the Lord Jesus Christ brings about that change. But, anyone who has been born again manifests this attribute of Love,

Because God is Love, and His children will show forth the same characteristic "We know that we have passed out of death into life (i.e. been born again), because we love the brethren" (I John 3:14).

2. We are children of God
The privileged position of the New Covenant saint far exceeds that of the Old Covenant saint (Matthew 11:11); the New Covenant saint is a child of God, whereas the Old Covenant saint was a servant only. God has called us into a family relationship with Himself and placed His Spirit within us so that we can say, "Abba! Father" (Romans 8:15) Abba is an Aramaic word meaning "father" and is used by little children when they speak to their fathers (in other words, Abba = Daddy).

In this way the Spirit of God in us is constantly reminding us that we are God's children. "And because you are sons, God has sent forth the Spirit of His Son into your hearts, crying, "Abba! Father!" (Galatians 4:6). Because we are born of God, we have Jesus as our elder brother; He is called the "first-born among many brethren"

(Romans 8:29), and we are among those brethren.

III. RECEIVING ETERNAL LIFE

In John 5:24 Jesus describes the transformation of the new birth as "passing out of death into life" (see also I John 3:14). When we were born again, we were born out of death and into life. The death we were born out of is spiritual death—the result of Adam's separation from God, who is the source of all life. The life which we were born into is the Life of God, or Eternal Life. God sent His Son into the world to give us Eternal

Life (John3:16). We received that Life by believing and accepting Jesus as our Savior (John 6:47). The moment we believed, God imparted His Life to our inner man, recreating us and causing us to be born again from death unto Life. Even as Adam became alive when God breathed into him the breath of Life, so we too became spiritually alive when God breathed into us His Eternal Life (I Corinthians 15:45).

A. WHAT IS ETERNAL LIFE?

God is the source of all life (Psalm 36:9; Jeremiah 2:13). He is called "the Living God" (Psalm 42:2; I Timothy 3:15) because He existed before anything else existed, and He was alive before anything had life. As the Living God, eternal and self-existent, God has absolute Life in Himself (John 5:26), and thus He is the source of all Life. Eternal Life (the Life of God) is the nature of God. "In Him was life, and the life was the light of men" (John 1:4). When we became partakers of God's nature (II Peter 1:4), we became partakers of Eternal Life.

1. Eternal life vs. "endless existence"
Eternal Life mustn't be confused with "endless existence." All men have endless existence, even those who don't believe on the Lord Jesus. Those who don't believe do not have eternal life, but they will exist for eternity separated from God (Matthew 25:41, 46).

Eternal Life is the nature of "the Living God." The result of having that nature is that we spend eternity in union with God, the source of Life.

2. When eternal life begins
When thinking of Eternal Life, some people suppose that it begins when they get to heaven. They believe that Eternal Life commences only after they have passed through "the Pearly Gates."

But the Bible says that those who believe have this Eternal Life now. "These things I have written to you who believe in the name of the' Son, in order that you may know that you have eternal life" (I John 5:13).

Eternal Life is imparted to us the moment we believe and accept the Lord Jesus as our Savior. "He who has the Son has Life!" (I John 5:12).

84

B. WHY JESUS CAME

"The thief comes only to steal, and kill, and destroy, I came that they might have life, and might have it abundantly" (John 10:10).

God didn't send Jesus into this world to start a new religion, or to establish a new code of ethics. Jesus came from the Father to give man life, the life he had lost through Adam's fall.

New religions and codes of ethics have never done anything to deliver men from bondage, because they can't do anything to change a man on the inside. Only Christianity imparts to man a Supernatural element—the Life of God When a Man receives the Life of God, it changes him; it alters his conduct and personality. When he believed, Paul was transformed from a violent persecutor of the church into an earnest Christian; God's Life came into him (Acts 9:1, 2, 20, 21). No sinner is so lost that the Life of God won't bring about a change. No case is incurable.

Receiving Eternal Life is the most miraculous event that can ever take place in any man's life. When God imparts His own nature to man, He is giving birth to a new creation.

IV. NEW CREATURES IN CHRIST

When a man is in Adam, he is dead (i.e. his spirit is dead to God, because in Adam all die (I Corinthians 15:22). But when a man turns to the Lord and is born again, he is in Christ. Paul said that he recognized all believers as being in Christ and not in the flesh (i.e. in Adam) (II Corinthians 5:16).

"Therefore if any man is in Christ, he is a new creature; the old things passed away; behold, new things have come" (II Corinthians 5:17). Any born-again believer is a new creature; his spirit, or inner man, has been recreated, and the old nature that he received from Adam at birth is done away with.

The term "new creature" refers to the result of the radical transformation that takes place when a man is reborn. This transformation occurs in a man spirit. A man's body is not born again (it will be redeemed when Jesus returns [Romans 8:23] neither is his mind born again (it must be renewed

(Romans 12:2). No, it is a man's spirit that is transformed instantaneously by the power and the Life of God. The inner man becomes a new creature the moment a person believes.

A. NEW CREATION = NEW NATURE

Adam's sin resulted in mankind receiving a sinful nature. This is the nature which drives men to sin and causes them to obey the impulses of Satan. This is the nature which makes men, "children of wrath" (Ephesians 2:3). The effect of the new birth is that this sinful nature is done away with and is replaced with a new nature. So completely new is this thing which God works in us, that the scriptures say we are "new creatures." We are not old creatures whom God has "fixed-up" enough to stand in His presence. God didn't "fix-up" our old nature; He destroyed it on the cross (Romans 6:6). He then put within us a new nature. This nature is not corrupted by sin, but is moved at the impulse of God's Spirit.

1. Created in His image
This new nature within us is nothing like the old nature. The old nature is corrupted and driven by sin. The new nature is created just like God, in all righteousness and holiness (Ephesians 4:22-24). When we receive this new nature, it means that we have become partakers of God's divine nature (II Peter 1:4). Thus, all the holy and righteous attributes of God are resident within us in the new creature (the new man).

We are children of our Father God, because God has caused us to be. Inwardly recreated in His very image; our spirits are endued with all of His righteousness and holy characteristics.

2. Complete re-creation
The work of our inward recreation is complete (Colossians 2:9, 10). God has already done all that He'll ever need to do within us to make us new creatures. Paul does not say that believers are "becoming" new creatures, but rather that they already are new creatures. If a person is not a new creature, then he is not in Christ, nor is he a child of God. Only new creatures can claim the privilege of being called "sons of God." Thus, anyone who is born again is now a new creature. This is a present-tense reality, not a future-tense expectation.

B. THE DUAL-NATURE FALLACY

In speaking of the birth and incoming of the new nature (new man), it is equally important to understand the death and removal of the old nature (old man). If any man is in Christ, old things (i.e. the old man) have passed away and new things (i.e. the new man) have come (II Corinthians 5:17). The scriptures show clearly that the coming of the "new" is made possible by the passing away of the "old."

No man can have two natures at the same time. As we have already said, one is either a child of God or a child of the devil; there is no middle ground (Matthew 12:30). Since the old nature makes a man a child of the devil, and the new nature makes him a child of God, it is obvious that the old nature and the new nature cannot coexist in any one person. These two natures are mutually exclusive. Unfortunately, some are of the mistaken impression that the new birth implants a new nature within us without removing the old. Thus, the new man and the old man are thought to exist side by side within us. This type of teaching readily acknowledges the new creature in Christ but does not understand that the old nature has been put to death and removed through Christ's work on the cross.

1. Paul's "wretched state"
One passage of scripture often used to support this "dual—nature" idea is found in Romans 7:14-24. Here Paul speaks of his state before regeneration, stating that he was sold into the slavery of sin. He speaks of the inner battle within a Jew who desires to keep the commandments of God, but cannot because of the sin which reigns in his mortal body.

It is believed that this describes the inner struggle between the "two natures" that supposedly dwell in all believers. People who believe this erroneously identify themselves with Paul's cry, "Wretched man that I am! Who shall deliver me from this body of death?" (Romans 7:24).

2. The reborn man's freedom from sin
That Paul is not speaking here of himself as a born-again believer is evident from Romans chapter 6 in which he says that any believer is free from the power of sin through Christ's death on the cross (Read Romans

6). The body of sin to which Paul refers in chapter 7 is the old man before it has been removed and replaced with a new nature. A "reborn" person no longer has an old nature within him (Romans 6:6).

C. INSTANT MATURITY?

Man is a triune being, made up of spirit, soul, and body. A man's spirit is that which contacts and responds to God (John 4:24); it is sometimes called the "inner man" (II Corinthians 4:16) or "the hidden person of the heart" (I Peter 3:4). The soul includes a man's mind and emotions. Both of these entities (spirit and soul) reside in a body.

Although the term "soul" is sometimes used to include spirit and soul (distinguishing them from the body), the scripture clearly makes a distinction between them (I Thessalonians 5:23; Hebrews 4:12). They are not one and the same.

When a man is born again, it is his spirit which becomes a new creature, undergoing an instantaneous change. This is not a process. The transformation of the spirit occurs the moment a man believes that Jesus is Lord. The same cannot be 'said, however, about the mind and the body. As we have already said, a man's mind doesn't get born again, and neither does his body. The mind of a believer must be renewed, and his body brought under control.

I. The need to conform
Paul calls upon each of us to be "transformed by the renewing of your minds" (Romans 12:2). He speaks of this transformation occurring as we gaze at the new creature we have become on the inside (II Corinthians 3:18). In Ephesians Paul refers to this outward transformation in conformity to the inward man as "growing up in Him" (Ephesians 4:14, 15).

It is important for us to realize that being a new creature in Christ (which is what we are) does not mean "instant maturity" in our outward walk. It does mean that all the power and potential for that Walk has already been placed within us by the new birth. We don't need to beg God to make us new; He's already done that. We need to begin walking in the light of what God has already accomplished within us.

2. The need to control

No matter how mature a Christian gets in his walk, he will always have to control the appetites of his body. The mighty apostle Paul (hardly one you would call immature) said that he buffeted his body and kept it under control (I Corinthians 9:27). The body (sometimes referred to as the flesh) must be controlled, and can be controlled when a believer allows his recreated inner man to dominate his body.

V. GOD'S INDWELLING PRESENCE

Not until righteousness has been established within us and we have been recreated (born again) can God fulfill His heart's desire to fellowship with us and indwell us through the person of the Holy Spirit.

The culmination of righteousness and the new birth is the Father and the Son coming into believers and remaining (abiding) in them (John 14:23).

A. GOD'S SPIRIT IN THE OLD TESTAMENT

Under the Old Covenant God's Spirit did not indwell men as He does in the New Covenant. This would have been impossible, since sin had not yet been removed. God anointed Old Testament believers by having His Spirit "come upon" them (Judges 3:10; 6:34; I Samuel 16:13). In this way God's chosen men were anointed and empowered for service.

1. Where God's anointing was

Not all Old Testament believers had the privilege of having God's Spirit come upon them. This was usually reserved for the King (or Judge), the Prophet and the Priest (I Samuel 10:6; II Chronicles 15:1; Exodus 28:1, 41).

These were specific men out of the nation of Israel, whom God chose to accomplish His will. The Priests were taken out of only one tribe of the twelve (the tribe of Levi), and then only one family of that tribe could minister as High Priest before the Lord (i.e. the house of Aaron). The King was a man of God's own choosing (Deuteronomy 17:15), and only descendants of that king's family could claim the privilege of God's anointing. Prophets were chosen by God as He saw fit and were anointed to proclaim God's message to His people (Jeremiah 1:5).

Thus, only on this specific group of people (i.e. King, Prophet, and Priest) did the Spirit of God rest. Not every believer under the Old Covenant could claim this privilege.

2. Where God's presence was

When God told Moses to build the Ark of the Covenant, He said that that would be the place where He would manifest His presence to the people (Exodus 25:21, 22). Throughout all 'The travels of the children of Israel, the Ark of the Covenant was identified with the presence of God. Where the Ark was, there, God was. When the Israelites took possession of the Promised Land, they set up the Ark and the tabernacle of worship in a place called Shiloh (Joshua 18:1). It was to Shiloh that men came if they wanted to hear from God or to do their service of worship (I Samuel 1:3), because this was where God's presence was in manifestation.

When David moved the Ark to the city of Jerusalem, the presence of God moved with it. God declares that Jerusalem is His city, chosen by Him as His habitation (Psalm 132:13, 14). This is not to say that God needs a building in which to dwell. Solomon himself said, as he dedicated the temple, "Behold, heaven and the highest heaven cannot contain Thee" (II Chronicles 6:18). But, God chose to show forth the glory of His presence in that place that is in the temple of Jerusalem (II Chronicles 7:1, 2).

B. THE PROMISE OF GOD

From what we have just read, we can see that the Spirit of God was not upon all men; it rested upon only a few. What's more, the children of Israel had to come to where the Ark was to worship God. But, God had better things in store for us! "And it will come about after this that I will pour out My Spirit on all mankind; even on the male and female servants, I will pour out My Spirit in those days "(Joel 2:28,29).

No longer will the Spirit of God be reserved for a special few; God will pour out His Spirit on all flesh (even slaves will be candidates for God's Spirit).

In this outpouring, however, the Spirit will not be upon people, but within them. "And I will put My Spirit within you" (Ezekiel 36:27).

Jesus said to His disciples before His death and resurrection that the Spirit that was then with them would soon be in them (John 14:17). This was profoundly illustrated upon Jesus' death, when the temple veil, which separated the people from the presence of God within the Holy of Holies, was ripped from top to bottom (Matthew 27:51), thus signifying that God's Spirit was no longer in a building, but was residing in men.

C. GOD'S SPIRIT IN THE NEW TESTAMENT

Unlike the Old Covenant, the New Covenant gives to every believer (not just a few) the indwelling presence of God's Spirit. Any man who is born again (a new creature) has God's Spirit living inside him. It is the Spirit of God who assures us of our redemption. "The Spirit Himself bears witness with our spirit that we are the children of God" (Romans 8:16). In fact, if a man does not have the Spirit of God dwelling inside, he is not saved: "But if anyone does not have the Spirit of Christ, he does not belong to Him" (Romans 8:9).

Every born again believer has God's Spirit residing inside him. When a man is justified before God by the blood of Jesus and becomes a new creature, then God can come and live inside him. We don't need to go to Jerusalem to worship God and experience His presence. We can now worship Him in spirit and in truth (John 4:20-23), because our bodies are now the temple of the Holy Spirit.

It is important for believers to understand that there is a vast difference between Old Covenant saints and New Covenant saints. Men under the Old Covenant had God's Spirit "come upon" them. This is very different from having the Spirit living within. What sets us apart from the men of the Old Covenant is that we have been made new creatures. Only in a new creature, holy and blameless before God, could God's Holy Spirit come to dwell . . .

This is why Jesus said that even though John the Baptist was the greatest prophet in the Old Covenant (Greater than Moses, Elijah, Elisha, etc.), the least in the Kingdom of Heaven was greater than he was (Matthew 11:11).

VI. SUMMARY—THE SUPERNATURAL, RADICAL, NEW BIRTH

The New Birth is totally the work of God through the Holy Spirit the only part which we play in it is to believe on the Lord Jesus Christ. This miracle of transformation which occurs on the inside of all who believe is what sets Christianity apart from every other religion or form of belief in the world.

Other religions try to alter a man's conduct sufficiently to bring about a change of his heart. But, faith in Jesus Christ alone will bring about a change in a man's heart, and only this change will alter his conduct. The New Birth does not occur as a result of works, but as a result of faith in Christ; it is not a work of the flesh, but a work of the Spirit. "That which is born of the flesh is flesh and that which is born of the Spirit is spirit" (John 3:5).The changes brought about by being born again are radical:

- You pass from death into life. (I John 5:24).

- You are delivered from the authority of darkness and translated into the kingdom of God's Son (Colossians 1:13).

- You received Eternal Life, the nature of God (Colossians 3:9, 10).

- You are made a new creature; old things pass away and new things come (II Corinthians 5:17).

- You have the indwelling presence of God's Spirit (I Corinthians 6:19).

LESSON FOUR
DAY ONE
THE NEW CREATION—BORN OF GOD STUDY QUESTIONS

1. There are two "births" that a man can experience; one every person experiences, the other not all experience. What are these two births?

    a. _____

    b. _____

2. I Corinthians 15:22 say, "For as in Adam all die, so also in Christ all shall be made alive." To what does the expression "in Adam" refer? What is the effect of a person being "in Adam"?

    _____

    _____

    _____

3. What is the New Birth, and why is it absolutely necessary for entrance into God's Kingdom?

    _____

    _____

    _____

    _____

    _____

4. Read Matthew 23:27. What did Jesus mean here? To what did He refer? How were the Jews, of Jesus' day as well as people today, deluded about this matter?

    _____

    _____

    _____

    _____

    _____

LESSON FOUR

DAY TWO

THE NEW CREATION—BORN OF GOD STUDY QUESTIONS

1. Briefly explain this statement: Man's basic problem is not what he does, but rather what he is! (Use scripture to support your answer.) Be sure to cover these points: the old nature inherited from Adam why being good isn't enough why God can't just "fix us up"

   _____

   _____

   _____

2. Why does the concept of "growth" not apply to the New Birth? Is there a place for growth in the Christian life? If so, how and where does it occur?

   _____

   _____

   _____

3. What is the difference between "endless existence" and "eternal life"? When does eternal life begin?

   _____

   _____

   _____

   _____

4. The New Birth ushers us into the family of God. What does it mean to you that you are a child of God? How will a deeper understanding of this fact affect your life?

   _____

   _____

   _____

   _____

LESSON FOUR

DAY THREE

THE NEW CREATION—BORN OF GOD STUDY QUESTIONS

1. Briefly explain the "dual nature" fallacy. To whom or what does Paul refer in the 7th chapter of Romans?

   _____

   _____

2. Ephesians 4:14,15 speaks of us "growing up in Him." How is it that believers grow up in the Lord? In what ways have you grown up in Jesus since you were born again?

   _____

   _____

3. Only three classes of people in the Old Testament had the privilege of having the Spirit of God upon them. Who were they?

   a. _____

   b. _____

   c. _____

   Under the Old Covenant, where did God usually choose to manifest His presence?

   _____

   _____

4. The Spirit of God could not indwell men under the Old Covenant. Why not?

   _____

   _____

   Why is it that you, under the New Covenant, can be indwelt by God's Spirit?

   _____

LESSON FOUR

DAY FOUR

THE NEW CREATION—BORN OF GOD STUDY QUESTIONS

1. Each of these scriptures gives us some information about the new birth. Briefly state the information given to us by each scripture.
    a. John 1:12,1 _____
    b. James 1:18 _____
    c. I Peter 1:23 _____
    d. I John 4:15 _____
    e. I John 5:1 _____

2. Read Ezekiel 36:26, 27. What two great promises does God make in this passage of scripture?
    a. _____
    b. _____

3. The promises made in Ezekiel 36:26,27 are already fulfilled in the life of anyone who believes on Jesus. What should you do if your emotions don't seem to match up with the reality of these promises?

    _____

    _____

    _____

4. Name five things that have happened to someone who has been born again.
    a. John 5:24 _____
    b. Colossians 1:13 _____
    c. I John 3:1 _____
    d. II Corinthians 5:17 _____
    e. John 14:7 _____

5. What immediate changes did you notice as a result of having accepted the Lord Jesus as your Savior, and being born again? What does the fact that you are born again mean to you right now?

_____

_____

_____

_____

_____

Lesson FIVE BAPTISM IN THE HOLY SPIRIT THE POWER OF GOD

Lesson FIVE BAPTISM IN THE HOLY SPIRIT THE POWER OF GOD

1. INTRODUCTION 103

II. BORN OF THE SPIRIT vs. BAPTIZED WITH THE SPIRIT.....104
   A. The Samaritan Revival 104
   B. Sauls Conversion— 105
   C. Cornelius' Conversion 105
   D. Distinct Works And Distinct MANIFESTATIONS.................105
      1. A well of water
      2. Rivers of living waters
   E. Old Testament Type of the Baptism in the Holy Spirit............106
   F. The Difference = Supernatural Power.....................................107

III. RECEIVING THE BAPTISM IN THE HOLY SPIRIT 107
   A. Only One Requirement
   B. A Free Gift..108
      1. Tarrying in Jerusalem
      2. Tarrying no longer necessary
   C. The Bible Evidence of the Baptism in the Holy Spirit............109
      1. The Day of Pentecost
      2. Cornelius' Household
      3. The Ephesians disciples
      4. Instances when tongues are implied
         a. The Samaritans
         b. Paul
   D. Tongues—A Supernatural River 111
      1. Edification
      2. Help in intercession
      3. Praying for the unknown
      4. Means of worship
      5. Public vs. private use

IV. THE DOORWAY TO THE SUPERNATURAL 113
   A. The Initial Evidence is Supernatural 114
   B. The Gifts of the Spirit...114
   C. The Supernatural Church..114

V. SUMMARY—THE SUPERNATURAL RIVER IN THE
BELIEVER 115

Lesson FIVE BAPTISM IN THE HOLY SPIRIT THE POWER OF GOD

1. INTRODUCTION

After Jesus was raised from the dead, He appeared to His disciples numerous times. For the space of forty days He was with them, teaching them about the kingdom of God (Acts 1:3). Yet, they still needed something from God before they would be ready to go out with the good news of Jesus' resurrection. Jesus said that they needed to be "baptized in the Holy Spirit."

Jesus told His disciples to wait for the promise of the Father "which you heard from me; for John baptized with water, but you shall be baptized with the Holy Spirit not many days from now" (Acts 1:4, 5). This "baptism in the Holy Spirit" was predicted by John before the beginning of Jesus' ministry. "He who is coming after me (Jesus) is mightier than I; He will baptize you with the Holy Spirit and fire" (Matthew 3:11, also read Mark 1:8, Luke 3:16, and John 1:33).

The promised day arrived ten days after Jesus' ascension on the day of Pentecost. On that day the Holy Spirit was sent from the Father by Jesus and all the disciples were "filled with the Holy Spirit" (Acts 2:4). This was the church's entrance into the supernatural realm, for the infilling of the Holy Spirit manifested itself in a supernatural way. The disciples began to speak with new languages (which they had never learned and which they did not understand), as the Holy Spirit gave them utterance, or ability to speak (Acts 2:1-4).

The disciples now had the same Holy Spirit that had indwelt Jesus during His ministry, and so they continued that supernatural ministry which He had begun. Thus, the baptism with the Holy Spirit was not the disciples' introduction to the kingdom of God, for they were already a part of that. It was, rather, their introduction into the supernatural, miracle—working power of God's Spirit. This remains today the factor that sets Spirit-filled believers apart: that is, the supernatural. Jesus intends all of His followers to walk in that supernatural power (John 14:12), and so promised all believers the "baptism with the Holy Spirit."

II. BORN OF THE SPIRIT vs. BAPTIZED WITH THE SPIRIT

At the new birth, the Holy Spirit comes to dwell inside a believer. The scriptures clearly state that anyone who is born again has the Spirit of God within them (Romans 8:9). He is there to teach, admonish, and to bear witness (John 14:26; John 16:8-11; Romans 8:16). However, when a person is born again he isn't automatically "baptized with the Spirit" (filled with the Spirit). Being "born of the Spirit" and "baptized with the Spirit" are two distinct manifestations of the Spirit of God. No man can be baptized with the Spirit until he has been born of the Spirit.

The distinction between being born again (conversion) and the baptism with the Holy Spirit can be seen in the accounts of this manifestation recorded in the book of Acts. On two occasions, believers were prayed for to receive the baptism (Or infilling) with the Holy Spirit, after they had been converted.

A. THE SAMARITAN REVIVAL

Read Acts 8:4-24

In this account we see that the gospel was being preached and believed in the city of Samaria. Those who believed what Philip was preaching were baptized in water, a sign of a person's entrance into the body of Christ. Jesus had said, "He who has believed and has been baptized shall be saved" (Mark 16:16).

Thus, these Samaritans were saved, members of the body of Christ, and "there was much rejoicing in that city" (Acts 8:8). And yet, they had not yet received the infilling of the Spirit. "For He (the Spirit) had not yet fallen on any of them" (Acts 8:16).

We can see from this passage that the new birth and the baptism in the Holy Spirit are not one and the same. The Samaritans were born again (saved) when they "received the Word of God" (Acts 8:14). But, this did not automatically give them the infilling of the Holy Spirit; that manifestation came when the apostles laid hands on them.

B. SAULS CONVERSION—

Read Acts 9:1-19

Saul's conversion (new birth) took place on the road to Damascus. This is evidenced by the fact that he addressed the risen Christ as "Lord" (Act 9:5) and then asked Jesus what He wanted Him to do Acts 20-:10) and obeyed Him. Saul (subsequently called Paul) said later that this was his witness of the resurrection (1 Corinthians 15:8). The man who was led blind into the city Of Damascus was a man who had witnessed and believed in the resurrected Christ and had submitted Himself to his Lordship.

But Saul, though converted, was not yet "filled with the Holy Spirit." Ananias came and laid his hands on him so that he might receive the baptism in the Holy Spirit (Acts 9:171. Again, we see a clear distinction between conversion (new birth) and the infilling (or baptism) in the Holy Spirit.

C. CORNELIUS' CONVERSION

There are instances where people are saved and filled with the Holy Spirit at the same time. Cornelius and his household had the Holy Spirit fail upon them as they were listening to Peter preach. No appeal was made to Cornelius to repent or confess: the Spirit fell upon him as he believed what Peter was saying about the Lord Jesus (Acts 10:44).

The new birth and the baptism in the Spirit can sometimes occur simultaneously; however, this does not mean that these two works of God are one and the same. If that were the case, the Samaritans (who had received the Word and been baptized in water) would not have needed to afterward receive the Spirit. If being born again meant the same thing as being filled with the Spirit, the convert Saul would not have needed Ananias to lay his hands on him to be filled with the Holy Spirit.

D. DISTINCT WORKS AND DISTINCT MANIFESTATIONS

Regeneration by' the Spirit and the baptism in the Spirit are two distinct works of the Spirit of God. They each result in a manifestation of the presence of God within the believer, but those manifestations are not the same. The difference is well illustrated in to statements made by Jesus and recorded in the gospel of John.

1. A well of water

"but whoever drinks of the water that I shall give him shall never thirst; but the water that I shall give him shall become in him a well of water springing up to eternal life"(John 4:14). In this statement Jesus refers to the indwelling of the spirit a man is born again. Water is often used in the Bible as a symbol of God's Spirit. The Spirit in a born-again believer is a well of water, bringing eternal life to those who possess it. The well is always there to quench a man's spiritual thirst for God and to sustain him. Every born-again believer has this well of the waters of God's Spirit within him.

2. Rivers of living waters

"He who believes in me, as the Scripture said, 'From his innermost being shall flow rivers of living waters'" (John 7:38). In this passage the water again refers to the Holy Spirit. But, now Jesus refers to the water as "rivers," not just a "well." This helps us to understand the difference between the presence of God's Spirit in those who are born again and those who are baptized in the Holy Spirit. In the former the Spirit's presence is like a well, but in the latter, the Spirit's presence is like rivers, which flow outward to give help and sustenance to others.

E. OLD TESTAMENT TYPE OF THE BAPTISM IN THE HOLY SPIRIT

In the Old Testament we see a type (a symbol) of the baptism in the Spirit when Israel crossed the Jordan into the Promised Land. Israel's passing through the Red Sea symbolized water baptism and our separation from the world (Egypt) (Exodus 14:22). But, before the nation could pass into the Promised Land, they had to cross another impassable physical barrier, the river Jordan. God parted the waters of this river as He did the waters of the sea (Joshua 3:14-17). The crossing of the Jordan by the miraculous power of God symbolizes the baptism in the Holy Spirit in the life of a believer.

That the crossing into the Promised Land does not symbolize our going to heaven when we die is seen clearly from the fact that Israel still had enemies to fight and defeat when she crossed the river. We will have no enemies to fight in heaven. While we remain on this earth, however, we do have an adversary (Satan) with whom we have to contend.

F. THE DIFFERENCE = SUPERNATURAL POWER

The Spirit of God indwells all who have Jesus as their Savior (Romans 8:9-16). God gives His Spirit to all His children to help and guide them, and to testify within them that they are indeed the children of God But, it is plain from the scriptures that this indwelling of the Spirit at the new birth is not the same as the baptism, or infilling, of the Spirit.

Those who are born again have the Spirit like water in a well, but those who are baptized In the Spirit have that Spirit like the waters of a river. The difference is not one of kind, but of volume and power. The baptism in the Spirit gives to a believer a greater manifestation of the presence of God and endues him with the supernatural power of God. "But you shall receive power when the Holy Spirit has come upon you" (Acts 1:8).

Being baptized in the Spirit is not a requirement for salvation or going to heaven. On the contrary, it is offered to those who believe (Acts 2:38), that is to those who are already born again. It is, however, a requirement for operating in God's supernatural power.

III. RECEIVING THE BAPTISM IN THE HOLY SPIRIT

Receiving the infilling or baptism in the Holy Spirit is not a complicated process. In fact, it is not a process at all. It is as simple as getting born again and receiving the Eternal Life of God. The gift of the Holy Spirit was poured out on the day of Pentecost and is available today to whomever will ask for it and receive by faith. Jesus said, "If you then, being evil, know how to give good gifts to your children, how much more shall your heavenly Father give the Holy Spirit to those who ask him?" (Luke 11:13).

There is only one preliminary requirement which a person must fulfill before he can be a candidate for the baptism in the Spirit: He must be born again, a believer in the Lord Jesus the infilling of the Spirit is not offered to sinners and those outside of God's kingdom. To sinners, God offers forgiveness and salvation, the way to be born again. The in—filling of God's Spirit is reserved for those who know Jesus as their Savior.

This is the **ONLY** prerequisite for receiving this blessing. Some Christians mistakenly believe that we must prove to God that we are holy or worthy enough to receive. God is thought to somehow look to see whether or not we deserve this blessing before He will bestow it. But the Bible calls the infilling of the Spirit a gift bestowed by the Father (Acts 1:4; 2:38) As with all gifts which God gives, this one is given on the basis of God's grace, and not on the basis of our goodness or worthiness.

The baptism in the Holy Spirit is not reserved for those Christians who are holy or mature enough to receive. Cornelius didn't have to wait until he was "mature" in the Lord before he received (Acts 10:44). The Samaritans didn't have to wait for years to receive; there was an urgency about them receiving which brought the apostles down from Jerusalem (Acts 8:14-16). This blessing from God has been made available to every Christian on the basis of the fact that they are born again.

B. A FREE GIFT

The baptism is just as much a free gift as is salvation and cannot in any way be earned. As with any gift which God bestows, this one must be received by faith. This means that God will give it when a person asks Him and will not wait until that person is holy enough or has "tarried" long enough to receive it. Some mistakenly believe that one must "tarry" for the infilling of the Holy Spirit before one can receive. They base this belief on Jesus' command to the apostles to "tarry ye in the city of Jerusalem, until ye be endued with power from on high" (Luke 24:49 KJV).

1. Tarrying in Jerusalem

Jesus told those disciples to "tarry" in Jerusalem to receive the Holy Spirit when He was sent. Up to that time, the Holy Spirit had not yet been given in fullness because Jesus had not ascended and sat at God's right hand. After the day of Pentecost, tarrying was no longer necessary, as subsequent accounts of the infilling of the Spirit bear out.

2. Tarrying no longer necessary

That this was a specific command, meant only for the disciples, is seen in the fact that Cornelius and his household did not in any way "tarry" for the Spirit; they received while they were listening to the message. The disciples in Ephesus received when Paul laid his hands on them, and there was no "tarrying" recorded there. The same is true of the Samaritan believers; they received when the apostles laid their hands on them.

C. THE BIBLE EVIDENCE OF THE BAPTISM IN THE HOLY SPIRIT

When a person is baptized in the Holy Spirit, there is a supernatural manifestation or evidence of that inward filling. That manifestation is called "speaking with other tongues (or languages)." Speaking with other tongues is simply speaking in a language which one has never learned and does not understand with his mind. Throughout the, book of Acts we find evidence that this sign accompanied the infilling of the Spirit.

1. The Day of Pentecost

On the day of Pentecost, the disciples were baptized in the Holy Spirit, just as Jesus had said they would be (Acts 1:5). When this event took place, they began to speak in other tongues. The languages they were speaking were not intelligible to them, but they were intelligible to the many foreigners which were in the city of Jerusalem at that time (Acts 2:5-7). This was, of course, a supernatural occurrence, signifying a miraculous work which had taken place within the believers who were gathered in the upper room. "And they were all filled with the Holy Spirit and began to speak with other tongues, as the Spirit was giving them utterance" (Acts 2:4).

2. Cornelius' Household

We have previously mentioned how that Cornelius was born again and baptized in the Spirit at the same time. The Holy Spirit "fell on them" as they were listening to Peter preach (Acts 10:44), and they were filled with the Spirit. Peter and his companions knew that these Gentiles had received the Spirit because they heard them speaking in other tongues. "And all the circumcised believers with Peter were amazed, because the gift of the Holy Spirit had been poured out upon the Gentiles also. For they were hearing them speaking with tongues and exalting God" (Acts 10:45, 46).

The Jewish brethren with Peter were truly amazed that Gentiles should receive the Holy Spirit (Acts 10:45), but they were convinced beyond any shadow of doubt that it was so because they saw the evidence of that infilling; the Gentiles were speaking in other tongues.

3. The Ephesians disciples

In his missionary travels Paul came across some disciples in Ephesus who had been taught incorrectly. They were not aware of the existence of the Holy Spirit. After Paul had straightened out their beliefs, he laid his hands on them for them to receive the infilling of the Spirit (Acts 19:1-5). "And when Paul had laid his hands upon them, the Holy Spirit came on them, and they began speaking with tongues and prophesying" (Acts 19:6).

Once again we see that the supernatural evidence of the Holy Spirit's infilling was speaking in other tongues, and in this case, prophesying as well.

4. Instances when tongues are implied

In the book of Acts, there are five recorded instances of people receiving the infilling of the Spirit (Acts 2:1-6; 8:14-17; 9:17; 10:44; 19:5-7). In the three that we have discussed, the evidence of speaking in other tongues is stated. In the remaining two, although speaking in tongues is not explicitly mentioned, study of the scriptures will show that it is certainly implied.

a. The Samaritans

The Samaritans received the infilling of the Spirit by the laying on of the apostles' hands. "Then they (the apostles) began laying their hands on them, and they were receiving the Holy Spirit" (Acts 8:17). The outward effect that receiving the Spirit had upon those believers was profound enough to catch Simon's attention (Acts 8:18, 19). This outward manifestation had to be more than just joy or exuberance, for these was already present before the apostles arrived (Acts 8:8). What Simon saw was so supernatural that it made him covet the authority to lay on hands as the apostles had done.

There is little doubt that the supernatural evidence which Simon witnessed was the same as the foreigners in Jerusalem had witnessed on the day of

Pentecost. It was the same evidence that the Jews in Cornelius' house had witnessed. The Samaritans were speaking in other tongues.

Paul was converted on the road to Damascus, when Jesus appeared to him (Acts 9:5, 6). But, he did not receive the infilling of the Holy Spirit until Ananias came and laid his hands on him (Acts 9:17). Although the scripture does not state here that Paul began to speak in tongues, Paul later told the Corinthian church that he did speak in tongues, more than them all (I Corinthians 14:18). Speaking in tongues was obviously a part of his Christian walk.

Since we have seen from the other four examples that speaking in tongues began when the believers received, there is no reason not to believe that Paul began speaking in tongues when he received.

D. TONGUES—A SUPERNATURAL RIVER

We can see from the above mentioned scriptures that the Bible evidence of the infilling of the Holy Spirit is speaking with other tongues (i.e. In other languages which are unknown to the speaker). This is an initial sign of the believer's has been baptized in the Spirit.

Again, this is not to say that tongues are an evidence of salvation; the Bible does not teach that. When a person is born again and receives the Spirit like a well of water within, the sign is the inner witness of the Spirit and an outward change reflecting what the new birth has wrought within. But, when a person is baptized in the Holy Spirit and receives the Spirit like rivers of living water, then the initial sign of those out—flowing, supernatural rivers is speaking in other tongues.

Speaking in tongues goes far beyond just initial evidence. The scriptures show that this supernatural manifestation became a part of the corporate life of the church (I Corinthians 12:7, 10), as well as giving great blessing in believers' personal lives (I Corinthians 14:4). The apostles spoke in tongues on the day of Pentecost as an initial sign of receiving the Holy Spirit, but this does not mean that that was the only time this phenomenon occurred in their lives. Paul indicated to the Corinthians that he frequently prayed in tongues (I Corinthians 14:18); he said this after he had received the infilling of God's Spirit.

There are several benefits to praying (speaking) in tongues which we can see from the scriptures.

1. Edification

"One who speaks in a tongue edifies himself" (I Corinthians 14:4). The word "edify" means "to build up." When a person prays in tongues, he is building himself up on the inside; his spirit is being strengthened. "But you beloved, building yourselves up on your most holy faith; praying in the Holy Spirit" (Jude 20) prying in the Holy Spirit is the same thing as praying in tongues. Those who pray in tongues build themselves up, because their spirits are praying directly to God. "For one who speaks in a tongue does not speak to men, but to God; for no one understands, but in his spirit he speaks mysteries" (I Corinthians 14:2). This is a divine, supernatural means by which our spirits can come into direct communication with God.

2. Help in intercession

By praying in tongues, we allow the Holy Spirit to pray through us prayers which are in accordance with the perfect will of God. "Likewise the Spirit also helpeth our infirmities; for we know not what we should pray for as we ought; but the Spirit itself maketh intercession for us with groanings which Cannot be uttered" (Romans 8:26 KJV). These "Groanings which cannot be uttered" include prayer in other tongues. "For if I pray in an unknown tongue, my spirit by the Holy Spirit within me prays, but my mind is unproductive" (I Corinthians 14:14 Amplified).

3. Praying for the unknown

There are times when we simply run out of words to say in prayer, or perhaps times when we don't even know where to begin to pray with our minds. In these cases the Holy Spirit is there to help us to pray (not to pray for us, but to help us). Praying in tongues enables us to pray in cases where we do not have complete understanding.

4. Means of worship

Speaking in tongues is also a way of giving thanks and praise unto God. In referring to a man who speaks in tongues during an assembly meeting, Paul says, "For you are giving thanks well enough, but the other man is not edified" (I Corinthians 14:17). The man who speaks in tongues gives thanks well; he himself is praising God, even though that particular giving of thanks does not edify the others around him, because they do not understand it.

5. Public vs. private use

All the benefits listed above (and there are certainly more than the ones listed) are the results of the private use of praying in other tongues. There is also a public use for speaking in tongues, and this is what the apostle Paul addresses in the fourteenth chapter of I Corinthians.

Many confuse Paul's statement, "Do all speak in tongues?" (The answer to this rhetorical Question is "No!"), to mean that not all are to use their prayer language (tongues) But, Paul is simply making a statement about the abuse of the public practice of speaking in tongues. If four or five men stand up in the middle of a service and simultaneously address the congregation in other tongues, then nobody in the congregation will be edified. "I thank God, I speak in tongues more than you all; however, in the church I desire to speak five words with my mind, that I may instruct others also" (I Corinthians 14:18, 19). Here Paul makes it plain that he speaks in tongues privately, but when he is addressing the assembly, he would rather speak in a known language so that all can understand and be edified. The private use of praying in tongues always edifies and helps the person who does it. But when addressing an assembly, one should not speak in tongues unless there is one to interpret, so that all may be edified. So we see that God's purpose is that we be edified—whether individually through the private use of tongues, or corporately through the public use of tongues and interpretation.

IV. THE DOORWAY TO THE SUPERNATURAL

Jesus' intention for His followers was that they should continue the ministry of preaching, teaching, healing, and deliverance that He had begun. He told His disciples that they would do the same works that He was doing and even greater works, because He was going to the Father (John 14:12). When He went to the Father, He sent the Holy Spirit (Acts 2:33) to empower the Church to do those works. Jesus told the disciples not to leave Jerusalem (to try to continue the earthly ministry He had started) before the Holy Spirit had come upon them (Acts 1:4). After they were baptized in the Holy Spirit,

Then they were witnesses "in Jerusalem, and in all Judea and Samaria, and even to the remotest part of the earth" (Acts 1:8). And wherever any of them shared the good news, the supernatural power of God was in manifestation (Acts 3:6,7; 5:12,15,16; 6:8; 8:7; 9:34,40; 14:9,10; 19:11,12).

A. THE INITIAL EVIDENCE IS SUPERNATURAL

As we have already seen, the initial evidence of the baptism in the Holy Spirit is speaking with other tongues. This is not a natural occurrence, but a supernatural one. Thus, it is fitting that this supernatural infilling of God's Spirit, to empower believers with supernatural power, should be accompanied by supernatural evidence. However, speaking in other tongues is only the beginning of a Spirit-filled believer's walk in the supernatural.

B. THE GIFTS OF THE SPIRIT

The gifts of the Spirit listed in I Corinthians 12 are all supernatural. They are not natural abilities, such as speaking ability or musical ability; these kinds of talents can be found in all men, even the unsaved. The gifts of the Spirit are the supernatural workings of God's Spirit through men. The baptism in the Holy Spirit will usher a believer into the working of these gifts.

C. THE SUPERNATURAL CHURCH

One of the striking characteristics of the early church was the fact that they moved in the realm of the miraculous. The miracle working power of God was not uncommon to the believers in that church. To them it was a matter of course that they should continue the ministry which Jesus had Begun, and that they should conduct it in the same manner as Jesus had conducted His earthly ministry (Matthew 4:23; Acts 5:14-16).

Jesus told them, "You shall receive power when the Holy Spirit has come upon you" (Acts 1:8). The kind of power Jesus was referring to was demonstrated in the apostles' ministry, as they went about preaching the word with signs and wonders following. But, God desires every believer to be endued with this same power. God wants all His children to be baptized with the Holy Spirit.

V. SUMMARY—THE SUPERNATURAL RIVER IN THE BELIEVER

The baptism of the Holy Spirit is for every born-again child of God. Every believer has the Spirit within like a well of water, but God wants every believer to also have the Spirit flowing out in power like rivers of water.

This river of living water flowing from within is the result of a person being baptized in the Holy Spirit. When the Holy Spirit is flowing out like a supernatural river, then supernatural things begin to take place Thus, when the disciples were filled with the Holy Spirit, they Began to speak in foreign Languages which they had never learned this was a supernatural occurrence. They then went out and began to perform the works of Jesus, and even greater works, because they had a supernatural river flowing from within.

LESSON FIVE

DAY ONE

BAPTISM IN THE HOLY SPIRIT—THE POWER OF GOD
STUDY QUESTIONS

1. When does the Spirit of God come to dwell within a believer? Is this the same as the baptism in the Holy Spirit? Explain.

_____

_____

_____

2. Briefly explain how the account of the conversion of the people of Samaria (Acts 8:4—24) shows us clearly that the new birth and the baptism in the Holy Spirit are two distinct and separate experiences with the Holy Spirit.

_____

_____

_____

3. Briefly explain how Saul's conversion (Acts 9:1-19) shows us the distinction between the new birth and the baptism in the Holy Spirit.

_____

_____

_____

4. In the gospel of John, what symbol does Jesus use to describe the role of the Holy Spirit in the new birth?

_____

in the baptism of the Holy Spirit?

_____

LESSON FIVE

DAY TWO

BAPTISM IN THE HOLY SPIRIT—THE POWER OF GOD
STUDY QUESTIONS

1. Using the symbolism that Jesus used in John 4:14 and John 7:38 explain the difference between those who have been born again, and those who have also been baptized in the Holy Spirit.

   _____

   _____

   _____

2. As we know, the Old Testament is filled with types and shadows which were fulfilled in the New Testament. What event in the travels of Israel is a type of our separation from the world through the new birth? What type foreshadows our being baptized in the Holy Spirit?

   a. _____

   b. _____

3. Who is eligible to receive the baptism in the Holy Spirit?

   _____

4. What would you say to a believer who felt that he wasn't mature or worthy enough to receive the infilling of the Holy Spirit. What scriptures would you share with that person?

   _____

   _____

5. Why is it no longer necessary to "tarry" for the Holy Spirit as the disciples did after Jesus' ascension?

   _____

   _____

   _____

LESSON FIVE

DAY THREE

BAPTISM IN THE HOLY SPIRIT—THE POWER OF GOD
STUDY QUESTIONS

1. The Bible records that the infilling of the Holy Spirit was accompanied by a super natural manifestation. What was that manifestation? Give three scriptures where this is recorded.

   _____

   Explain what this manifestation is.

   _____

2. List four benefits of speaking in tongues.

   a. _____

   b. _____

   c. _____

   d. _____

3. Define the word "edifies," and explain why speaking in tongues accomplishes this in the life of a believer. (Give scripture to support your answer).

   _____

   _____

4. What is the difference between the private and public use of tongues?

   _____

   What does the public use of tongues always require?

   _____

   What is the common purpose behind both public and private use of tongues?

   _____

LESSON FIVE

DAY THREE

BAPTISM IN THE HOLY SPIRIT—THE POWER OF GOD
STUDY QUESTIONS

1. How have you personally been blessed by the private use of tongues in your own life?

   _____

   _____

   _____

   _____

   _____

2. What one word describes what we receive after being filled with the Holy Spirit? Give scripture reference.

   _____

3. Write a short testimony concerning your baptism in the Holy Spirit. When and how did it happen? (If you did not receive the baptism in the Holy Spirit, would you like to right now?)

   _____

   _____

   _____

   _____

   _____

   _____

   _____

   _____

   _____

   _____

   _____

   _____

   _____

Lesson SIX THE RENEWED MIND: TRANSFORMED BY THE WORD OF GOD

Lesson SIX THE RENEWED MIND: TRANSFORMED BY THE WORD OF GOD

1. INTRODUCTION 125

II. MAN—A THREE PART BEING 125
  A. Man Is A Spirit...126
  B. Man Has A Soul 126
  C. Man Lives In A Body 127
  D. Three-Fold Redemption 128

III. WHY YOU NEED TO HAVE YOUR MIND RENEWED 128
  A. The Corruption of the Soul 129
    1. Walking by sight
    2. Living by emotions
  B. Your Mind Doesn't Get "Born Again" 130
  A. The True Reflection 131
    1. The mirror of the Word
    2. Power to act
    3. Simple facts
    4. Unchanging reality
  B. Gaze Intently Into The Mirror...133
    1. The forgetful hearer
    2. The effectual doer
    3. Looking and acting
  C. The Truth Will Make You Free 134
  D. By The Power of the Holy Spirit...134

V. SUMMARY—THE MIND OF CHRIST 135

Lesson SIX THE RENEWED MIND: TRANSFORMED BY THE WORD OF GOD

1. INTRODUCTION

When a man accepts Jesus as his Savior and Lord, he is born out of darkness into light. He is delivered from Satan's authority and translated into the Kingdom of God. This is not a process of gradual development from darkness to light, or from death to life. It is an instantaneous change within; God recreates him, and he becomes a "new creature" in Christ.

However, there is growth and development which takes place in the Christian life. Peter tells us to "grow in grace and in the knowledge of our Lord and Savior . . ." (II Peter 3:18). The new birth does not mean that those who are born again are instantly mature. There is a process which must begin to take place within the life of every believer. Paul calls this process a "transformation"; we are outwardly changed (our actions and walk) into the image of the new creature which God has made us to be on the inside (II Corinthians 3:18). "And be not conformed to this world, but be transformed by the renewing of your mind" (Romans 12:2). When a Christian is transformed by the renewing of his mind, he "grows up in all aspects into Him" (Ephesians 4:15).

II. MAN—A THREE PART BEING

Before proceeding any further in our study of this transformation, we would do well to investigate the three-fold nature of man. Man is made up of three parts: spirit, soul, and body. The spirit and soul of a man are distinct from his body. This can be understood from simple observation. What is not quite so obvious is that the spirit and the soul of a man are also distinct entities.

There are instances where the scriptures use the word "soul" collectively of both spirit and soul. When it is thus used, "soul" refers to that part of man which is unseen and eternal (read Matthew 10:28 & Acts 2:27). But, the spirit and the soul of a man are not one and the same. "Now may the God of peace Himself sanctify you entirely; and may your spirit and soul and body be preserved complete, without blame at the coming of our Lord Jesus Christ" (I Thessalonians 5:23).

"(Hebrews 4:12). For the word of God is living and active and sharper than any two-edged sword, and piercing as far as the division of soul and spirit" These scriptures make a clear distinction between spirit and soul equating the two will only lead to confusion.

A. MAN IS A SPIRIT

God is a spirit (John 4:24), and when He created man in His own image, He created him a spirit. So man also is a spirit. Although we see with our eyes a man's body, yet the real man is on the inside. Peter calls this the "hidden man of the heart" (I Peter 3:4). Paul calls it the "inner man" (II Corinthians 4:16). These expressions (hidden man, inner man) refer to the same thing; they refer to a man's spirit.

When Adam sinned and fell from the glory of God, it was his spirit that died. "But from the tree of the knowledge of good and evil you shall not eat, for in the day that you eat from it you shall surely die" (Genesis 2:17). The death that God was speaking of was spiritual death. This is the condition that is radically changed by the new birth. When a man is born again, he becomes a totally new creature. The man on the inside, the hidden man of the heart, becomes new. All the old things which kept a man separated from God and in bondage passed away (II Corinthians 5:17).

The new birth takes place in the heart—the inner man That new man is made in the likeness of God in all righteousness and holiness (Ephesians 4:24). Since God is a spirit, it is a man's spirit which is in contact and communion with the Father. "The Spirit Himself bears witness with our spirit that we are the children of God" (Romans 8:16). It is through our spirits that we have fellowship with God and are guided and directed by Him. So this was the part of man that was totally recreated.

B. MAN HAS A SOUL

The word "soul" (when used in distinction from spirit) refers to a man's mind (intellect) and his emotions. The effect of the fall upon man's mind and emotions was one of corruption. It caused men to think and to feel in a way that was contrary to the way God thinks. "For my thoughts are not your thoughts, neither are your ways my ways; declares the Lord" (Isaiah 55:8).

Before a man is born again, his mind and emotions are controlled largely by his unregenerate spirit. Thus, they are programmed according to the standards of the world. Worldly ideals are natural to this kind of mind; because that is the way it has been trained. The new birth gives to man a completely new heart, one that is aligned with God and desires to do His will. As we have said, this is an instantaneous happening. But man's mind and Emotions (his soul) must be renewed through the Word of God, by the power of the Holy Spirit. This renewing of the mind is the process of maturing in which a believer's mind and emotions are trained to come into line with God and His Spirit.

C. MAN LIVES IN A BODY

While our spirits have been reborn and our minds are being renewed, the fact remains that we still live in mortal bodies and will do so until Jesus returns. At the return of Jesus, all those who are still alive will be "changed, in a moment, in the twinkling of an eye, at the last trumpet" (I Corinthians 15:51-53). But, this putting off of mortality for immortality will not occur until the second coming of Jesus.

The body is the tent, the dwelling place of the spirit and the soul of man. The apostles Paul and Peter both clearly expressed this conviction in their epistles. For we know that if the earthly tent which is our house is torn down, we have a building from God, a house not made with hands, eternal in the heavens We are of good courage. I say, and prefer rather to be absent from the body is to be at home with the Lord" (II Corinthians 5:1, 8). "And I consider it right, as long as I am in this earthly dwelling, to stir you up by way of reminder, knowing that the laying aside of my earthly dwelling is imminent" (II Peter 1:13,14).

In both these passages, it is plain that the apostles saw their bodies as simply the abodes of their spirits. The real "person" was not their physical body, but the spirit and soul within that body.

While he was still alive and present in his body, Paul said that he did something with his body. I buffet my body and make it my slave, lest possibly after I have preached to others, I myself should be disqualified" (I Corinthians 9:27). Every Christian has a responsibility to control the appetites of his body and make his body his slave. A Christian who spends his entire life on the earth ruled and dominated by his body will be disqualified from the prize. The prize here is not eternal life. Eternal life is received at the new birth. The prize is the reward that every believer will receive from God for the deeds done while in the body (II Corinthians 5:10).

D. THREE-FOLD REDEMPTION

Just as man is three-fold in nature, his redemption is three-fold also. A man's spirit is totally and completely redeemed when he accepts Jesus as his Savior and Lord. That work happens **instantaneously**. A man's mind and emotions must be renewed by the Word of God. This is **the process of Christian maturity.** A man's body will not be redeemed from mortality (inevitable physical death) until **the second coming** (when Jesus returns to catch His church away). (Mortality means that this present body must die. It does NOT mean that this body must suffer with sickness while we live in it. Isaiah 53:3, 4 and Matthew 8:17 explicitly state that freedom from sickness is part of the atoning work of Christ. While a Christian lives out his life in this mortal body, he has a covenant right to do so **free from sickness!**)

III. WHY YOU NEED TO HAVE YOUR MIND RENEWED

The new birth results in a new creature, made in the likeness of God. That new creature is infused with the divine nature of God (II Peter 1:4), and has been made the righteousness of God (II Corinthians 5:21). If you are born again, you ARE a new creature. God's power has been manifested on your behalf and has recreated you on the inside. But there is still a transformation which must take place in the life of every believer. That transformation is a process. It happens as a believer begins to have his mind and emotions renewed to the reality of who he is in Christ, and all that Christ has done for him.

"As he reckons in his soul, so is he" (Proverbs 23:7). The way a man thinks of himself will largely determine the state in which he will live. If his mind and emotions see only defeat and misery, then that is what he will experience. A renewal has to take place in which the believer begins to see himself as God sees him. Then the state in which he lives will be in accordance to the Word and will of God.

A. THE CORRUPTION OF THE SOUL

A believer's mind and emotions need to undergo a transformation because they were corrupted. This corruption happened because the soul was dominated by an unregenerate spirit, alien to God. Before being born again, a man's mind and emotions are programmed to think, feel, and respond in a way that is contrary to God and His Word.

His soul learned how to sin. It learned how to be depressed and feel sorry for itself. In other words, it learned the ways of this world and was programmed according to its dictates.

1. Walking by sight

One of the ways in which the soul of man is trained is in walking by sight. Most men's minds are very well trained to believe only what they can see or experience through the physical senses. To the unrenewed mind, what is seen constitutes reality. There is no reality other than what can be seen. Thus, the unrenewed mind (the "natural man") is unable to comprehend the things of God because they appear to be foolish and unreal (I Corinthians 2:14).

2. Living by emotions

The unrenewed mind has also been trained to live by emotions. People often equate their identity with how they are feeling at that particular moment. If they feel unloved, they assume that they are unloved. If they feel rejected and alienated, they believe that rejection and alienation are realities. Generally, they are using their emotional state as their reference point to determine who they are and what they have we can see how the emotions of a man and the truth of God's Word are not always in agreement. The Bible says that we are accepted in the beloved (Ephesians 1:6), that we are more than conquerors (Romans 8:37), that no weapon formed against us shall prosper (Isaiah 54:17). But, many believers don't "feel" like they are accepted by God, or that they are conquerors. They often "feel" rejected and defeated.

The unrenewed mind, when given the choice between believing what is seen (i.e. physically experienced) and believing the Word of God, will always choose to believe what is seen.

B. YOUR MIND DOESN'T GET "BORN AGAIN"

Jesus said, "You must be born again" (John 3:7). The experience to which He referred takes place in the spirit of a man. A man's spirit is translated from darkness to light, and from death unto life. This change takes place in a moment; the instant a man receives Jesus as his Lord.

The same cannot be said of a man's mind and emotions. The mind and emotions of a man do not get born again. They must be renewed by the Word of God. There is often an emotional response to the new birth within a person. But, this cannot be equated with a renewed mind. Even after the spirit has been recreated, many old thought patterns still remain. The process of erasing old thought patterns is called "renewing the mind."

"And do not be conformed to this world, but be transformed by the renewing of your mind, that you may prove what the will of God is, that which is good and acceptable and perfect" (Romans 12:2). Paul said to believers (new creatures), "Don't be conformed to this world."It is possible for a person who is a new creature to be outwardly conformed to the former manner of life and thinking. This conformity is an ongoing process of moving away from God and His life.

There is no such thing as a stationary spiritual condition for a believer. One is either moving toward God, in conformity to him, or away from God, in conformity with the world. We live in a world in which there is a current that goes the opposite direction from God. If a believer chooses to "relax," he'll be swept along by the current, being gradually conformed to this world and its standards. There is no standing still in God. One is either being transformed by the renewing of the mind, or he is being conformed to this world.

But, as a person's thinking is changed into God's way of thinking (i.e. as his mind is renewed), an outward transformation begins to take place. This transformation is also an ongoing process, in which the inward work of the new birth begins to be outwardly manifested in a believer's life-style. In this process a believer's thoughts and actions (i.e. his outward walk) change, becoming more and more Christ-like. The righteous inner man can be seen by others when he is allowed to manifest himself through a person's character and personality.

Read II Corinthians 3:18 and James 1:22-24

A. THE TRUE REFLECTION

If you are born again your thoughts and emotions are not always a true guide or reflection of who you are on the inside. Sometimes Christians become discouraged because they feel that their contrary emotions and thoughts are a reflection of who they really are. But, there is only one true reflection of who a believer is, and that reflection doesn't come from a person's emotions. It comes from the Word of God.

1. The mirror of the Word

"But we all, with unveiled face, beholding as in a mirror the glory of the Lord, are being transformed into the same image from glory to glory, just as from the Lord the Spirit" (II Corinthians 3:18). When a person looks into a mirror, he sees himself. But, this scripture says that we behold the glory of God as in a mirror. The reason is that this mirror reflects the glory of God within us. We see there the glory of the new creation which God has made us to be.

The mirror is the Word of God. God's Word gives us a clear picture of who we are in Jesus Christ and all the things that belong to us in Him. As we gaze into that mirror and contemplate the hidden man of the heart, a transformation (begins to take place. We begin to become like the image that we are beholding. Our outward walk begins to conform to what we see in the Word of God.

2. Power to act

"For you were formerly darkness, but now you are light in the Lord; walk as children of light" (Ephesians 5:8). The power to walk as a child of the light will come as the believer settles in his mind and heart that he is a child of the light. The settled assurance that one is a new creature can only come from looking steadfastly into God's Word. Without the mirror of the Word, we would be the slaves of ignorance. The only reflection we would have of ourselves would be one of mere outward appearance.

3. Simple facts

Here are some simple Bible facts concerning who you are in Christ and all the things that you have in Him.

- **You are a new creature in Christ (II Corinthians 5:17).**

- **You are a partaker of God's divine nature (II Peter 1:4).**

- **You have been given everything pertaining to life and godliness (II Peter 1:3).**

- **You are free from the power of sin (Romans 6:6).**

- **You are redeemed from the curse of poverty and sickness (Philippians 4:19; Matthew 8:17).**

- **You are more than a conqueror in Jesus (Romans 8:37).**

- **You are filled with God's love (Romans 5:5).**

- **You have been seated with Christ in heavenly places (Ephesians 2:6).**

- **You have been blessed with all spiritual blessings (Ephesians 1:3).**

These statements about us from the Word of God are a true reflection of who we really are. They show us the way in which God Himself sees us, because they are a commentary on the work that He accomplished on Calvary. These scriptures actually mirror to us the hidden man of the heart, the spirit on the inside that was recreated when we were born again.

4. Unchanging reality

Even though a person's emotions and thoughts about him can change from day to day, yet the Word of God never changes. And so, the reflection of the hidden man of the heart will always be the same, no matter what a believer may feel like. Whether a believer feels accepted or rejected, the Word always says that he is accepted in the beloved. Whether he feels like a loser or a conqueror, the Word always says that he is more than a conqueror.

God's Word is consistent; it never changes. So, too, is the inner man; he doesn't change from day to day, but is always the same. He is always free, redeemed, healed, filled with God's love, blessed, and more than a conqueror.

B. GAZE INTENTLY INTO THE MIRROR

In James 1:22-24 we again find the allegory of the mirror. Here also, the mirror is the Word of God in which a man sees his reflection. But in this passage of scripture, there are two men described. One is a man who hears the word, but does not act upon it (the forgetful hearer); the other is a man who hears the word and does act upon it (the effectual doer).

1. The forgetful hearer

This man looks at himself in the mirror and then goes his way, immediately forgetting what manner of man he was. Casual and intermittent reading of the Word of God has had little lasting effect upon that man, and he's forgotten what he heard. Many believers are like this man. They read the Word of God (that mirror which reflects who they really are), but quickly forget the image that they saw there. They are "forgetful hearers." They are very easily swayed from their conviction by contrary emotions or thoughts, because they look into the mirror of God's Word only casually and intermittently. Thus, they rarely act in a way which reflects that new man, because they have quickly forgotten what he looks like.

2. The effectual doer

This man looks intently into the perfect law of liberty. His gaze is not diverted by other thoughts and emotions, but he abides in the Word. Because he continues to look into that mirror, there seeing more and more clearly who he is in Christ, he doesn't become a forgetful hearer. He is a doer of what he sees.

This man is able to act like the man that he sees on the inside. One cannot be an effectual doer until he is an intent gazer. When a person has been consistently looking in the mirror and meditating on what is seen there, he'll find it easy to act like the man that he is observing. He'll find it natural to believe like the new creature that he really is.

3. Looking and acting

We saw in II Corinthians 3:18 that as we behold in the mirror (i.e. the Word of God) the glory which God has placed in us, then we are changed (outwardly) into that glorious image. One must have a clear picture of who that new creature is before he can begin to act like him. But as that picture begins to come into focus, there is a time for the believer to **ACT.**

All the gazing in the world is useless unless a person makes a quality decision to behave like the new creature that he sees.

Many believers get the cart before the horse. They try to act like a new creature before they know that they are one. You cannot act like a new creature in order to become one. That is impossible. The only thing that will enable a person to walk like a new creature is to know that God has made him one already. Then again, some Christians get the horse and cart in the correct order, but fail to put the horse in motion. As the image of the inner man is getting clearer and clearer (and it will come into focus more and more with time), there comes a responsibility to act. The believer must put faith in the fact that what the Word says about him is true and **ACT** on it.

C. THE TRUTH WILL MAKE YOU FREE

"If you will abide in my word, then you are truly my disciples; and you shall know the truth, and the truth shall make you free" (John 8:31, 32) There is liberty and freedom from bondage in knowing the truth about your self. If we abide in God's Word (that mirror which reflects our new inner nature), then we'll know the truth of who we are in Christ Jesus.

And, that knowledge will have an effect upon us. It will set us free to act like new creatures. The knowledge that comes through abiding in the Word is knowledge that will renew your mind. It will change the way you think, from the world's thought patterns to God's thought patterns. When God said, "For My thoughts are not your thoughts, neither are your ways my ways," He didn't mean that He wanted it to continue that way. God's desire is that our thinking comes into line with His thinking, so that our ways will come into line with His ways.

D. BY THE POWER OF THE HOLY SPIRIT

We do have a part to play in this transformation, since we are responsible to look intently into the mirror (Word) and then act according to what we see there. But, we must never lose sight of the fact that the actual transformation taking place is a work of the Holy Spirit (Titus 3:5). The Holy Spirit is the One who renews our minds by showing us what the Word really promises us (I Corinthians 2:12). The Holy Spirit is the one who transforms us into the new creation image reflected in the Word. We are " . . . transformed into the same image from glory to glory, just as from the Lord the Spirit" (II Corinthians 3:18).

V. SUMMARY—THE MIND OF CHRIST

The unrenewed mind is one that believes only what is seen. It walks by sight, and not by faith. Thus, it is contrary to God and His ways (Isaiah 55:8). While the mind is in fellowship with an unregenerate spirit, it learns to think in ways which are not God's ways. It is trained to deny the power of God; it is trained to fear and to doubt. When a man is born again, his spirit is recreated, but his mind remains largely the same as it was before. So a process must take place in which that unrenewed mind is renewed to the principles of God's Word. As the new believer meditates in the scriptures and fills his mind with God's thoughts, his unrenewed mind will begin to change. It will begin to think in line with God, in line with faith and hope and love; it will begin to think like the mind of Christ.

As the believer's mind is renewed, his actions and his outward walk will also begin to change. He will begin to act more and more like Jesus, because he has been made in that image. As he sees clearly that righteous new creation, as it's reflected in the mirror of the Word, he'll find it easy to act in accordance with the image he's steadfastly beholding.

LESSON SIX
DAY ONE
THE RENEWED MIND—
TRANSFORMED BY THE WORD OF GOD STUDY QUESTIONS

1. After a person is born again, what needs to begin to take place in his life?

   _____

   _____

2. What are the three parts of man? Give scripture references for each.

   a. _____

   b. _____

   c. _____

3. Why did the apostle Paul call his body an "earthly tent"?

   _____

   _____

   _____

4. Is your body "born again"? What must you, as a believer, do with your body, and why?

   _____

   _____

5. The apostle Peter speaks of "the hidden man of the heart," and Paul talks about "the inner man." To what do both of these expressions refer? How is the inner man affected by the new birth? How do you know that this has taken place in you?

   _____

   _____

   _____

LESSON SIX

DAY TWO

THE RENEWED MIND—

TRANSFORMED BY THE WORD OF GOD STUDY QUESTIONS

1. What are two ways in which people with unrenewed minds have been trained?

   a. _____

   b. _____

2. Why must we have our minds renewed? In the light of your answer, explain what Paul says in I Corinthians 2:14. Give an example of the type of person which this describes.

   _____

   _____

   _____

3. How will an unrenewed mind respond to physical circumstances which are contrary to the truth of God's Word?

   _____

   _____

   _____

4. Give an example from your own life which illustrates, "As he reckons in his soul, so is he" (Proverbs 23:7). Based on your knowledge of God's Word, have you changed any thought patterns or actions that were "conformed to this world" (Romans 12:2)?

   _____

   _____

   _____

   _____

LESSON SIX
DAY TREE
THE RENEWED MIND—
TRANSFORMED BY THE WORD OF GOD STUDY
QUESTIONS

1. Explain why there is no such thing as a "stationary spiritual condition" for a believer.

   _____

   _____

2. How is God's Word like a mirror to us?

   _____

   _____

3. Read II Corinthians 3:18. Why is it that when we look into the mirror of God's Word, it reflects the "glory of God"?

   _____

   _____

4. List ten things which you see about yourself in the mirror of the Word. (Give scriptures.)

   a. _____
   b. _____
   c. _____
   d. _____
   e. _____
   f. _____
   g. _____
   h. _____
   i. _____
   j. _____

LESSON SIX
DAY FOUR
THE RENEWED MIND—
TRANSFORMED BY THE WORD OF GOD STUDY QUESTIONS

1. As the image of who we are in Christ comes into focus, what are we responsible to do? What does the Bible call that person who fails to fulfill this responsibility (Matthew 7:24-27)?

   _____

   _____

   What does the Bible call that person who fails to fulfill this responsibility (Matthew 7:24-27)?

   _____

2. Read Romans 12:1, 2. Briefly explain what this passage means to you, in light of all that you have learned in this lesson.

   _____

   _____

   _____

   _____

   _____

3. Jesus said in John 8:31, 32, "If you abide in my word, then you are truly disciples of Mine; and you shall know the truth and the truth shall make you free." How (in what ways) has the Word of God set you free?

   _____

   _____

   _____

   _____

   _____

Lesson SEVEN FREEDOM FROM SIN: ALIVE TO GOD

Lesson SEVEN FREEDOM FROM SIN: ALIVE TO GOD

I. INTRODUCTION 145

II. DEAD TO SIN 146
   A. The Old Man 146
     1. Born into death
     2. The unregenerate state
     3. Exposed by the Law
   B. Crucified with Christ 148
     1. The body of sin made powerless
     2. Dead to the world
   C. Made Alive to God 149
     1. Delivered and transferred
     2. Willing and working

III. WALKING IN FREEDOM 150
   A. Freedom to Choose 151
     1. The truth
     2. Servants of righteousness
   B. Put To Death the Deeds of the Body 153
     1. Controlling fleshly desires
     2. The war of the flesh and the spirit
     3. The fruit of obedience to the spirit
   C. Temptation 154
     1. Resist condemnation
     2. Respond immediately
     3. "Flee immorality"
   D. Walk By the Spirit 156
   E. The Wages of Sin 157
     1. Sin destroys faith
     2. Sin destroys fellowship with God
   F. We Have an Advocate 158

IV. WATER BAPTISM 159
   A. Water Baptism in the New TESTAMENT 159
   B. Water Baptism in Perspective...160
      1. The point of separation
      2. Identifying with Jesus

V. SUMMARY—WALKING IN THE LIGHT 161

Lesson SEVEN FREEDOM FROM SIN: ALIVE TO GOD

I. INTRODUCTION

We have already seen in Lesson 3, that God justified us through the sacrifice of Jesus. God forgave us all our sins and made us to be the righteousness of God in Christ (II Corinthians 5:21). This righteousness (right-standing with God) is based, not on works, but on faith. There were no good works which we did which made us worthy to receive. God declared us righteous on the basis of His mercy and grace, as we put faith in His crucified and risen Son.

Every believer is righteous on the inside, because he has become a partaker of God's divine, righteous nature (II Peter 1:4). Righteousness is infused into the very being of every Christian. This is why we can come boldly before God's throne. This is why we can have the abiding presence of His Spirit with us continually. Without our having been made righteous: we could not be called the sons of God (I John 3:1). God is righteous, and those who are born of Him have the same nature that He has.

But, righteousness means more than just right-standing with God. "Little children, let no one deceive you; the one who practices righteousness is righteous, just as He is righteous" (I John 3:7). John did not write this statement to condemn, or to make people feel that they are unsaved. He simply states that those who are righteous on the inside have the power and ability to **ACT** righteously. The idea of **ACTING** right cannot be separated from the New Testament concept of righteousness.

"For we are His workmanship, created in Christ Jesus **for good works**, which God prepared beforehand, **that we should walk in them**" (Ephesians 2:10). We were not created by good works, but we were created for good works. God's desire is that the righteous, holy nature that is within us (that nature which enables us to stand before God unashamed) begins to manifest itself in our outward walk. It is abnormal for a righteous new creature to continue to walk under the bondage of sin. God has made the way clear for ALL believers to walk completely free from sin's domination in their lives. Indeed, He has called every believer to this kind of walk. "But like the Holy One who called you, be holy yourselves also in all your behavior" (I Peter 1:15).

II. DEAD TO SIN

Read Romans 6:1-7

God will not give a command to His people unless He has also given them the ability to fulfill that command. God's call to believers is for them to live holy lives, free from the bondage of sin. But, God has also given to every believer the ability to walk above sin and sinful habits. The new birth resulted in a new man, one that is not sinful. On the contrary, that new man is perfect, made in the very image of God. God has enabled us to walk free from sin's power: by putting to death the thing within us that drove us to sin, and by placing within us a powerful and righteous new nature.

Many believers try to fulfill this call to holiness without having a clear understanding of the work that God has done in their inner man. The work of the cross cleansed us from the guilt and condemnation of sin. Jesus' shed blood washed us clean from all our sins. Yet if that were all that was done, we would be forgiven, but still dominated by an evil inner nature which would make us sin. But, the work of Calvary not only removed the guilt and condemnation of sin, it also removed the source of sin within us. The evil drive within us that made us slaves to sin was done away with on the cross. We must have a clear understanding of this fact of redemption, so that we may walk in all the liberty God has purchased for us.

A. THE OLD MAN

"Knowing this, that our old self (old man) was crucified with Him, that our body of sin might be done away with, that we should no longer be slaves to sin" (Romans 6:6). The thing that kept us enslaved to sin was the "old man." This "old man" (or old creature) had to be killed in order for us to be freed from sin's power. This was the part of us that was crucified with Jesus 2,000 years ago. "I have been crucified with Christ, nevertheless I live" (Galatians 2:20).

1. Born into death

Our old man was that part of us that was dead to God before we were born again. When Adam sinned in the Garden of Eden and fell from the glory of God, he was born out of life into death. He became a sinful creature, ruled and dominated by an inner nature which drove him to sin.

This helpless state was passed onto all of Adam's descendants (Psalm 51:5; I Corinthians 15:21, 22).

Unsaved men are thus left with an evil inner nature, which Paul calls the "old man." The old man cannot be reformed or rehabilitated. This is the reason that humanistic philosophy fails to bring about any real change in men.

Trying to reform the "old man" will only end in failure. There is only one effective way to deal with the evil inner nature: it must be killed.

2. The unregenerate state

In Romans 7:14-25, Paul describes the state of an unregenerate man who is ruled by his sinful nature. Here we find a vivid picture of what it is like to be dominated by an old man that is yet alive and well. The man Paul describes:

a. Is sold into bondage to sin (Romans 7:14).

b. Does the very thing that he hates to do (Romans 7:15).

c. Is unable to do the good that he wants to do (Romans 7:18).

d. Is a prisoner of the law of sin in his body (Romans 7:23).

e. Serves the law of sin in his flesh, even though it is contrary to the law of God which his mind acknowledges (Romans 7:25).

f. Is a WRETCHED MAN! (Romans 7:24).

Careful reading of the previous chapter of Romans (chapter 6) will show clearly that Paul is not referring to himself as a Christian in this particular passage. He is describing himself before he was saved. Paul, as an unregenerate Jew, knew what was the right thing to do, but was unable to do it. The reason he could not do the things that he knew were right, was because the old man had not yet been done away with in Christ. There was a power within that drove him to sin that he could not overcome.

3. Exposed by the Law

God exposed man's real inner condition (which was a sinful inner nature) by giving him the Law. The Law was given to show man once and for all that the problem within could only be dealt with through Jesus Christ. The Law was holy, righteous, and good (Romans 7:12), but because of man's sinful nature, it resulted in death. "Therefore did that which is good become a cause of death for me? May it never be! Rather it was sin, in order that it might be shown to be sin by effecting my death through that which is good, that through the commandment sin might become utterly sinful" (Romans 7:13).

The old man within took the Law, which was good, and turned it to evil. The Law could not change the inner condition of man; it only exposed it for what it really was. Thus, God showed sin to be "utterly sinful," without any hope of redemption apart from Jesus Christ. God's solution to this dilemma struck a death blow at the very root of the sin problem in man. As we have said, death was the only way out of this trap, and this is exactly what God did through His Son.

B. CRUCIFIED WITH CHRIST

Paul said that the old man was crucified with Christ (Romans 6:6). That inner disposition to sin, which left men helpless, was put to death with Jesus. This was the beginning of our identification with His redemptive work on the cross. Paul was so acutely aware of the reality of this vicarious death that he told the Colossians, "For you have died, and your life is hid with Christ in God" (Colossians 3:3).

The key to our being freed from the slavery of sin is our death with Jesus. "He who has died is freed from sin" (Romans 6:7). Because we are now dead (that is, our old man is dead), sin is no longer our master.

1. The body of sin made powerless

Once the old man is crucified with Jesus, then the "body of sin" is made ineffective. "For we know that our old self was crucified with Him so that the body of sin might be rendered powerless, that we should no longer be slaves to sin" (Romans 6:6 NIV). This gives us insight into what happens when the old man is crucified. The body of sin, that thing which drove us to sin, was "rendered powerless!"

The old inner nature always went in a way that was contrary to God and His way; it was a power within us which made it impossible for us to overcome sin. But, the Bible says that the old man was killed, put to death on the cross. Since the old nature is DEAD, it no longer has the power to dominate us. "If any man be in Christ, he is a new creature; the old things have passed away" (II Corinthians 5:17).

2. Dead to the world

The death of our old nature on the cross means that we are totally separated from the world and its sinful principles. "But may it never be that I should boast, except in the cross of our Lord Jesus Christ, through which the world has been crucified to me, and I to the world" (Galatians 6:14). We are separated from the world and all that it stands for, just as much as a physically dead man is separated from this physical world (i.e. his physical surroundings).

A man who is physically dead no longer has any relation to this physical world. It doesn't affect him, because he is no longer a part of it. The government would not think to try to collect taxes because the system no longer has any relation to him. He is dead. He is not a part of this world. In the same way, believers are dead to the earthly principles of the world, because that old man who made them a part of this world system is no longer alive. He was crucified with Jesus. And so every believer is "dead to sin"; he is no longer a part of sin, nor is sin a part of him.

C. MADE ALIVE TO GOD

Our identification with Christ didn't end on the cross. "Now if we have died with Christ, we believe that we shall also live with Him" (Romans 6:8). Paul is not speaking here of the resurrection on the last day. He refers to the fact that just as Christ was raised from the dead, we too were made alive spiritually. "... As Christ was raised from the dead through the glory of the Father, so we too might walk in newness of life" (Romans 6:4). We were crucified with Christ, in order that we might walk in newness of life, alive to God and free from sin.

"Even when we were dead in our transgressions, (He) made us alive together with Christ . . . , and raised us up with Him, and seated us with Him in the heavenly places, in Christ Jesus" (Ephesians 2:5,6). Here we see the completion of our identification with Christ: Crucified with Him! Made alive together with Him! Rose up with Him! Seated in heavenly places with Him!

1. Delivered and transferred

Just as the death of the old man separated us from the world so our being made alive to God makes us a part of His kingdom. "For He delivered us from the domain of darkness, and transferred us to the kingdom of His beloved Son" (Colossians 1:13). We are part of His kingdom, because He has made us new creatures and filled us with His own holy and righteous nature. Our new nature is the nature of God (II Peter 1:4).

We were once alive to sin and dead to God, because our old man was still alive. But now we are dead to sin and alive to God, because the old nature is dead (separating us from sin and the world) and a new nature has been given to us (which puts us in contact with God).

2. Willing and working

When we were alive to sin, we did by nature the things which sin desired. But now that we are alive to God, there is within us not only the power, but also the desire to do what is right before God.

"For it is God who is at work in you, both to will and to work for His good pleasure" (Philippians 2:13) our new nature within is made in the image of God. The new man has the ability to do God's good pleasure; but he also has the will to do God's good pleasure. We not only have the power to do the will of God, but we can do it without grudging or complaining.

III. WALKING IN FREEDOM

When we begin to realize all that has been done for us through the death and resurrection of Christ, it becomes evident that sin is NOT the normal Christian life! God didn't put the old man to death to have us continue to live in slavery to sin. He didn't crucify us with Christ to see us flounder helplessly in sinful habits.

God set us free on the inside, so that we could live in complete mastery over sin and over the enticements of the flesh and the devil. God's desire is for every one of His children to rise above sin and live a life of purity and integrity. "For God has not called us for the purpose of impurity, but in sanctification" (I Thessalonians 4:7; also read I Thessalonians 4:3). Sanctification signifies our separation from the world by virtue of our manner of life.

"How shall we who died to sin still live in it?" (Romans 6:2). To Paul, a Christian bound by sin was an abnormality. It was a denial by the believer that God had done anything inside him at all. Since he knew that the price for a believer's complete liberty from sin had already been paid, Paul was constantly exhorting Christians to live according to what God had done on the inside of them. He told the carnal Corinthians: "Or do you not know that your body is a temple of the Holy Spirit who is in you, whom you have from God, and that you are not your own?" (I Corinthians 6:19). "I, therefore, the prisoner of the Lord, entreat you to walk in a manner worthy of the calling with which you have been called" (Ephesians 4:1). "For you were formerly darkness, but now you are light in the Lord; walk, as children of light" (Ephesians 5:8).

A. FREEDOM TO CHOOSE

'Paul gives us a vivid picture in Romans 7:14-25 of a man who 'is bound by sin. The man described there does not have the freedom to choose to do what is right. He is hopelessly trapped into doing the wrong thing. But, the death of the old man in us means that we have been given back the freedom to choose between righteousness and sin. This was the freedom of choice that Adam had in the garden. The old nature was done away with, and the driving force of sin was stripped of its power to dominate us.

So, the choice between sin and righteousness is before every believer. He is called upon to make this choice on a daily basis, as various temptations come his way He can choose to follow the inclination of his regenerate spirit, or he can choose to follow the inclination of his flesh. God has given His children the freedom to choose.

1. The truth *

After Paul tells us that we are dead to sin, he goes on to enumerate the choice that is before us. "Therefore do not let sin reign in your mortal body that you should obey its lusts, and do not go on presenting the members of your body to sin as instruments of unrighteousness; but present yourselves to God as those alive from the dead, and your members as instruments of righteousness to God" (Romans 6:12,13. All the power to walk above sin has been given to us, but it is then up to us as to whether we will "let sin reign in our mortal bodies."

When confronted with a temptation or enticement to sin, remember that you do have a choice. Satan will always try to convince you that falling into sin is inevitable, that there is no choice. Often he will quote the Bible (out of context) to support his lie. For example: "For the good that I wish, I do not do; but I practice the very evil that I do not wish" (Romans 7:19). This verse, describing a man before he is born again, is often used to try to convince ignorant believers that falling into sin is an inevitable way of life for them.

The truth is, however, that you are free to choose between sin and righteousness', because the old man is dead. If this were not the case, then Paul's exhortation for us not to "let sin reign in our mortal bodies" would be Paul exhorts us to choose because we do indeed have that freedom through the redemptive work of the cross.

2. Servants of righteousness

You are the servant of the one to whom you present yourself and the members of your body. If you present your body to sin, to obey its dictates, then you are sin's servant. But, if you present yourself-to God on a daily basis, then you are a servant of God and of righteousness (Romans 6:16, 19).

"I urge you therefore, brethren, by the mercies of God, to present your bodies a living and holy sacrifice, acceptable to God, which is your spiritual service of worship" (Romans 12:1). Because God has restored to us our free will (i.e. freedom to choose), we can present ourselves to God, as servants of righteousness we are given this option.

B. PUT TO DEATH THE DEEDS OF THE BODY

"So then, brethren, we are under obligation, not to the flesh., to live according to the flesh for if you are living according to the flesh, you must die; but if by the Spirit you are putting to death the deeds of the body, you will live" (Romans 8:12,13). We are **NOT** obligated to obey the lusts of the flesh. As we have said, we are **FREE** to choose not to sin. However, there is something which we as believers must do with our bodies. We have been freed from sin. But this does not mean that every desire or thought that comes into our heads is godly and should be obeyed. Christians need to learn to put to death the deeds of the body.

Because the body has not yet been redeemed from the fall (remember that this will not occur until Jesus' return, we need to control it. Even Paul said that he kept his body under control, so that he wouldn't be disqualified (I Corinthians 9:27).

1. Controlling fleshly desires

Since our bodies (flesh) are still mortal (as yet unredeemed), there remains in them desires that are contrary to God. Before we were saved, we had no control over those desires, because the old man within us empowered the flesh. But, now the dominating power of sin has been removed. We are still left, however, with a body (or flesh) which likes to do things which are against God's ways.

Remember, our spirits are the part of us that get born again. Our minds are renewed by the Word of God. But, our flesh is neither born again nor is it renewed. It must be kept under control. This controlling of fleshly desires will get easier and easier as a person's mind is renewed to the fact that sin has no real dominion over his will.

2. The war of the flesh and the spirit

The desires of the flesh and the desires of our recreated spirit are the source of the inner conflict with sin that all believers experience. "For the flesh sets its desire against the (S) spirit*, and the spirit against the flesh: for these are in opposition to one another, so that you may not do the things that you please" (Galatians 5:17).

153

Every believer has a recreated inner man that likes to obey God. But that inner man is housed in a body that likes to disobey God and to go the way of the world and so, you have the desires of the Flesh warring against the desires of your inner man. But if you choose to follow after the spirit, then the deeds of the flesh will be put to death in your mortal body. "But I say, walk by the spirit, and you will not carry out the desire of the flesh" (Galatians 5:16).

Some mistakenly believe that this inner conflict against sin (the desires of the flesh) is really a fight between the "old man" and the "new man," who are simultaneously housed in the body. The struggle is thought to be between two equally powerful forces. But, the scriptures do not bear this idea out. The old man was crucified, and the body of sin rendered powerless. As we have already seen, the old man and the new man cannot coexist in one body. One is a new creature, or he is an old creature; he can't be both at the same time.

3. The fruit of obedience to the spirit
Every believer has the power to say NO! to sin and temptation. The deeds of the body (flesh) are no match for the recreated inner man, because the dominating force behind the flesh (i.e. the old man) is dead. But, Christians must use their free will and choose to obey their spirits rather than the flesh. They must choose to keep their bodies under control and put to death evil deeds.

The fruit of doing this is sanctification, that righteous outward walk that God desires to see all His children experiencing (Romans 6:19, 22). The result will be a life above sin, free from sinful habits that destroy faith and fellowship with God.

C. TEMPTATION

Every believer, while he remains in his "earthly tent," will experience temptation. The desires of the flesh, excited by the suggestions of Satan (the tempter), will try to pull a believer away from God and into sin (James 1:14, 15). The key to overcoming temptation, and not succumbing to it, is in acknowledging who we are in Christ. "Even so consider yourselves to be dead to sin, but alive to God in Christ Jesus" (Romans 6:11). When Paul says "consider," he does not mean "pretend as if it were so." He means that we are to meditate on the fact that we are dead to sin and its power. We are to set our minds on the things of the spirit, and not on the things of the flesh. "Set your mind on things above, not on the things of the earth" (Colossians 3:2).

1. Resist condemnation

In dealing with temptation, one must recognize that it is not a sin to be tempted! Often, Christians feel condemned because they have a lustful or a hateful thought. The enemy will plant an evil thought in the mind of a believer, and then accuse that believer of being a vile and sinful creature.

If one allows himself to be condemned by a temptation then his next thought will be: "Thinking it is as bad as doing it, so you might as well indulge." But, having a tempting thought is **NOT** the same as carrying it out.

The Bible says of Jesus that He " . . . has been tempted in all things as we are, yet without sin" (Hebrews 4:15). Jesus was tempted in every way, and those temptations were not considered sin. He was victorious over every temptation and was without sin. It is no more a sign of failure or defeat for a believer to be tempted than it was for Jesus to be tempted. A Christian's response to temptation should be one of resistance instead of condemnation.

2. Respond immediately

It is not a sin to be tempted. But, temptation will inevitably lead to sin if evil thoughts are entertained for any length of time. Dwelling on the things of the earth and of the flesh will only lead to a fall into sin (James 1:14, 15). Temptation must be dealt with quickly, the moment it arises. The longer a person waits to deal with those temptations, the harder they will find it to resist.

Jesus' response to temptation was immediate and effective. Whenever the devil brought a temptation before Him, He responded, "It is written!" (Luke 4:4, 8, 12) He didn't wait and think about what the devil had said; He refuted the devil's lies with the Word of God.

Paul tells us to meditate and dwell on the fact that we are now dead to sin, that sin does not have the power to dominate us. This must always be our response to temptation, one that affirms that we are dead to old sinful ways and are now alive unto God and righteousness. When a believer is tempted to sin, his response should be vocalized: "No! I am dead to sin. Sin does not rule me. I am alive to God in all righteousness and purity!"

3. "Flee immorality"

No believer will ever reach the level of maturity in which he cannot be tempted. As long as he remains in his earthly body, he will have to deal with temptation. This means that he cannot expose Himself to the "gravitational pull" of sin. It is one thing to be tempted by the enemy. It is quite another to place yourself in a position where temptation is inevitable. "Put on the Lord Jesus Christ, and **make no provision for the flesh, in regard to its lusts**" (Romans 13:14). Staying around sin and its pull will always result in a fall.

The believer is free from sin. But, that does not mean that he is free to frequent places of sin or to consistently fellowship with sinners. "Bad company corrupts good morals" (I Corinthians 15:33). To be free from sin means that you are **FREE TO RUN AWAY!** Paul said, **"Flee** immorality" (I Corinthians 6:18), and "Now **flee** youthful lusts" (II Timothy 2:22). The redemptive work in you has given to you the ability to "abstain from fleshly lusts, which wage war against the soul" (I Peter 2:11). But, we must be careful that we "do not give the devil an opportunity" (Ephesians 4:27) by placing ourselves in a position where he can easily tempt us.

D. WALK BY THE SPIRIT

The Bible makes it clear that believers have a responsibility to set their minds on the things of the spirit and not on the flesh. "For the mind set on the flesh is death, but the mind set on the Spirit is life and peace" (Romans 8:6). Whether or not a person sets his mind on the flesh or on the spirit is up to the individual; God will not do it for us. But, we are told that if we do set our minds on the spirit, and walk by the spirit (that is, the new creature God has made us to be), then we will not fulfill the desires of the flesh (Galatians 5:16).

The power to act like the new man that we are on the inside comes as we meditate upon God's Word that identifies that new man (II Corinthians

5:17, 21). As a believer acknowledges who he is in Christ and sets his mind upon the things of the spirit, rather than on the things of the flesh, he'll find that the desires of the flesh don't have any power to overcome him.

E. THE WAGES OF SIN

Sin is destructive! One look around at the state of the world will suffice to show beyond doubt that sin always results in death and destruction. "For the wages of sin is death" (Romans 6:23) That is why it is dangerous for a Christian to take a relaxed or neutral attitude toward sin. Sin always results in misery, as it did at the fall when Adam sinned. It should be regarded as a deadly enemy, because that is what it is. "Do not be deceived, God is not mocked; for whatever a man sows, this he will also reap. For the one who sows to his own flesh shall from the flesh reap corruption, but the one who sows to the Spirit shall from the Spirit reap eternal life" (Galatians 6:7, 8).

1. Sin destroys faith
Sin destroys faith in the believer. It is impossible to receive from God through faith, when one is living in sin (I John 3:22). The principle of faith stated in Mark 11:24 will not work unless the principle of Mark 11:25 are followed. "Therefore I say to you, all things for which you pray and ask, believe that you have received them, and they shall be granted you. And whenever you stand praying, forgive; if you have anything against anyone; so that your Father also who is in heaven may forgive you your transgressions" (Mark 11:24, 25).

In Joshua chapter seven is the story of Israel's defeat at Ai. The children of Israel had just soundly defeated the people of Jericho and went forward in the same faith to destroy Ai. Yet they were defeated by the inhabitants of that city. When inquiry was made, it was found that there was sin in the camp; some of the soldiers had taken spoils from Jericho, as was strictly forbidden by the Angel of the Lord (Joshua 6:18). It was not until sin was eradicated from the people that Israel could go up and defeats Ai (Joshua 7 & 8).

2. Sin destroys fellowship with God
Sin also destroys fellowship with the Father. One cannot have fellowship with God and walk in sin at the same time. "If we say we have fellowship

with Him and yet walk in the darkness, we lie and do not practice the truth" (I John 1:6). If a believer continues to violate his conscience with sin, he will not have any confidence before God, and fellowship will remain dead until that sin is renounced. If he persists in that sin, his heart will become hardened, and the awareness of God's presence will drift farther and farther away.

Believers cannot afford to take sin with a light attitude. God has called us to a life of holiness before Him, because He knows the destructive power of sin. God tells us to live uprightly before Him, because He knows that that is the only path of life and peace (Romans 8:6). Any parent would strictly forbid his child from playing in a pit that was filled with rattlesnakes. He would do so, not because he didn't want the child to have any "fun," but because he wants the child to live! In exactly the same way, God calls His children to live a life above sin, for He is fully aware of sin's destructive power.

F. WE HAVE AN ADVOCATE

"My little children, I am writing these things to you that you may not sin. And if anyone sins, we have an Advocate with the Father, Jesus Christ the righteous" (I John 2:1). If a believer does sin, it is not the end. Even if a person has been bound for years with the same sinful habit, God's Word proclaims forgiveness and release! Jesus is our Advocate with the Father, for His blood has forgiven us all our sins. "If we confess our sins, He is faithful and righteous to forgive us our sins and to cleanse us from all unrighteousness" (I John 1:9).

God will forgive us every time we sin, if we will confess it before Him and ask forgiveness. This is not meant as a license to sin. It is meant to get us back into fellowship with God, and back into a position of faith and confidence from which we can walk free from sin's bondage. No one will ever walk free from sin if he is laboring under condemnation. Condemnation doesn't help a person to overcome sin; it drives him further into it, because it drives him away from God.

"There is therefore now no condemnation for those who are in Christ Jesus" (Romans 8:1). Unless a believer understands this principle, he'll never walk free from sin. If a person falls in some sin, he must ask forgiveness, and then get up again. A baby would never learn to walk if it decided to stay on the ground after a fall. If a baby falls while it is learning to walk, it will get up and go again. Similarly, if a believer falls in some sin, he must repent and get up again, confessing that there is no condemnation to those who are in Christ Jesus.

IV. WATER BAPTISM

Water Baptism has its roots in the ritual washing prescribed in the Old Testament (Exodus 30:17-21; Leviticus 11:25). By the time of John the Baptist, some of these washings had developed into a practice called "baptism." The word "baptize" literally means "immerse in water," and this is what John was doing in the river Jordan. John's baptism was one of repentance. It was the people's sign that they had renounced sin. This explains John's sharp rebuke for the hypocrites, who came to be baptized; he rebuked them because they had not turned from sin (Matthew 3:7, 8).

John's baptism was a baptism of the Old Covenant, and it was very different from the baptism which Jesus charged His disciples to perform, before His ascension (Matthew 28:19). John's baptism symbolized for that time the people's act of repentance and purification. The kingdom of heaven was at hand, so the people prepared themselves (Matthew 3:2). The New Covenant baptism which Jesus commanded symbolizes a miraculous, inward transformation, in which all sins are washed away (Acts 22:16).

A. WATER BAPTISM IN THE NEW TESTAMENT

Jesus gave to His disciples the command to make disciples of men and to baptize them (Matthew 28:19). Throughout the book of Acts we find that the disciples obeyed this command. As soon as a person had been saved, he was baptized in water. The Philippian jailer was baptized the very night that he accepted Jesus as Lord (Acts 16:33). The Ethiopian eunuch was baptized as soon as he was converted (Acts 8:3638). Cornelius, the Roman centurion, was baptized when the disciples recognized that he had been born again and had received the Holy Spirit (Acts 10:47, 48). In each one of these cases, new converts were baptized in water in obedience to the command of the Lord Jesus.

Jesus' command was that His disciples baptize "in the name of the Father and the Son and the Holy Spirit" (Matthew 28:19). However, in the book of Acts, it is recorded that people were baptized in the Name of Jesus (Acts 8:16; 10:48; 19:5). This has been an issue of considerable controversy. Suffice to say that the merit of water baptism is in the faith that the individual puts in it, and not the formula by which it is done. The Corinthian's were caught up in this same kind of controversy. But in his letter to them, Paul simply retorted, "For Christ did not send me to baptize, but to preach the gospel" (I Corinthians 1:17). Paul wasn't belittling the meaning of baptism; he was just putting it in proper perspective.

B. WATER BAPTISM IN PERSPECTIVE

"Or do you not know that all of us who have been baptized into Christ Jesus have been baptized into His death? Therefore we have been buried with Him through baptism into death . . ."(Romans 6:3, 4) When a person is baptized, he is identifying himself with the death, burial, and resurrection of Jesus (Colossians 2:12). Water baptism is a person acting out his faith in the fact of the new creation. When a person is born again and the old man crucified, he is separated from the world and its values. Identifying with Jesus in baptism is then making a statement of the fact that we are no longer a part of this world. We are in the world, but not of the world (John 17:15, 16).

1. The point of separation

In I Corinthians 10:1 we are told that the passing of the children of Israel through the Red Sea was a type or shadow of baptism (I Corinthians 10:1, 2). To the children of Israel, the Red Sea was their point of absolute separation from Egypt and their former life of bondage. Egypt is symbolic of the world and of our former bondage to sin.

So, water baptism is to be a clear point of separation in the life of every believer. It signifies the death of the old man, which connected us to the world's system, and the birth of the new man, which connects us to God Himself. "Therefore we have been buried with Him through baptism into death, in order that as Christ was raised from the dead through the glory of the Father, so we too might walk in newness of life" (Romans 6:4).

2. Identifying with Jesus

The apostle Peter likened baptism to the experience of Noah, in which Noah and his family were saved from a society which was under the judgment of God. The people in the ark were saved from destruction because they were separated from that wicked society. Through water baptism we cease to identify with the world that crucified Jesus and unite ourselves with Christ's body and family.

If you are a believer, and you have not been water baptized, do so. You need to make this step of obedience to the Lord Jesus. You need to affirm by a physical and public act that you no longer consider yourself a part of this world system. You are now a child of God, and so not of this world.

If you have been water baptized, mix faith with what you have done and walk in the light of your being a new creature in Christ.

V. SUMMARY—WALKING IN THE LIGHT

God has made every provision for us to walk uprightly before Him. He put to death the power that forced us to sin and placed within us a righteous new nature. There is no reason for any believer to walk in anything but complete victory and mastery over sin and sinful habits. God created His Church for victorious living, not for constant defeat at the hands of sin. However, it is up to the individual as to whether or not he or she will make the quality decision to walk according to the new man, rather than according to the dictates of sin and the flesh.

If a believer chooses to walk according to the flesh, death in one form or another will be the result. But, if that believer chooses to walk according to his recreated spirit (the inner man) then the result will be life and peace. "But if we walk in the light as He Himself is in the light, we have fellowship with one another, and the blood of Jesus His Son cleanses us from all sin" (I John 1:7).

FREEDOM FROM SIN—ALIVE TO GOD STUDY QUESTIONS
LESSON SEVEN
DAY ONE

1. We have already established the fact that righteousness means right standing with God. But, there is more to it! What else is involved in the New Testament definition of righteousness? What scripture clearly points this out?

   _____

   How is this distinct from the concept of "righteousness by good works"? (Ephesians 2:10).

   _____

2. List six attributes of the man Paul describes in Romans 7:14-25.

   a. _____   d. _____
   b. _____   e. _____
   c. _____   f. _____

   What kind of man does this passage refer to: born again or unregenerate? Why? (Give scriptures.)

   _____

   _____

3. How does the fact that the old man was crucified enable us to live free from sin? (Give scriptures.)

   _____

   _____

4. What are the four basic aspects of our identification with Christ? (Give scriptures for each.)

   a. _____   c. _____
   b. _____   d. _____

FREEDOM FROM SIN—ALIVE TO GOD STUDY QUESTIONS
LESSON SEVEN
DAY TWO

1. Define "sanctification."

   _____

   _____

   _____

   _____

2. As believers, we now have freedom to choose. What is the choice
   that confronts us every day? Explain.

   _____

   _____

   _____

   _____

3. Our spirits are born again; our minds are being renewed. But, neither
   of those things happens to the flesh. What are we as believers
   instructed to do about the flesh?

   _____

   _____

   _____

   _____

4. Why is there a conflict between the flesh and the spirit? What are
   we to do about this conflict?

   _____

   _____

   _____

   _____

   _____

FREEDOM FROM SIN—ALIVE TO GOD STUDY QUESTIONS
LESSON SEVEN
DAY THREE

1. Prove from the scriptures that it is not a sin to be tempted.

   _____

   _____

   _____

2. Why is it dangerous for a Christian to entertain temptation? What must our response to temptation be? Explain.

   _____

   _____

   _____

3. Anew believer tells you that he still goes to parties with his old friends, but, he does not drink or use drugs like everyone else. He feels that it's all right to go to such places, because he is now free from the power of sin. What Biblical counsel would you give this brother?

   _____

4. What is the wages of sin?

   _____

   What two things in the life of a believer will be destroyed if sin is openly practiced?

   a. _____

   b. _____

   Why?

   _____

   _____

   _____

FREEDOM FROM SIN—ALIVE TO GOD STUDY QUESTIONS
LESSON SEVEN
DAY FOUR

1. What do you do if you have committed a sin, and are feeling condemned about it?

   _____

2. Why does condemnation not help Christians to stop sinning?

   _____
   _____
   _____

3. Why is a Christian's water baptism like Israel's passage through the Red Sea?

   _____
   _____
   _____

4. Summarize the main point in three of the following passages of scripture:

   Ephesians 5:8; ll Timothy 2:19; I John 2:6; II Corinthians 7:1; I Corinthians 15:34; Romans 6:12; Colossians 2:5 (Choose only three.)

   Explain how these admonitions affect and apply to your life as a Christian.

   a. _____
   _____
   _____

   b. _____
   _____
   _____

   c. _____
   _____
   _____

Lesson EIGHT FAITH THE REST OF GOD

Lesson EIGHT FAITH—THE REST OF GOD

I. INTRODUCTION 171

II. RECEIVING THE PROMISES OF GOD 171
   A. Redeemed From the Curse of the Law..............................172
      1. The all-inclusive redemption
      2. in this life
   B. Partaking of our Redemption 173
      1. Plugging into the power source
      2. The touch of faith
      3. Failing to possess
   C. Releasing the Power of God.....................................175

III. FAITH—EVIDENCE OF SPIRITUAL REALITY.....................176
   A. God's Unseen Reality...176
      1. The unseen spiritual realm
      2. Walking by the superior reality
      3. Temporal vs. eternal reality
      4. Abraham's assurance
   B. God's Word Reveals the Unseen 178
      1. Revelation knowledge
      2. Spiritual perception
   C. Faith That Pleases God...179
      1. The problem of Thomas—faithlessness
      2. The example of Mary—believing God's Word
   D. Possessing God's Promises Through Faith 180
      1. Wondering & wishing
      2. Bible faith

IV. FAITH—A POSITION OF REST 181
   A. Revelation of God's Love 182
      1. Faith responds to grace
      2. Having faith in God's faithfulness
   B. Faith Is of the Spirit...183
      1. Faith is not intellectual (mental assent)
      2. Faith is not emotional excitement (feelings)

V. SUMMARY—THE FAITH THAT PLEASES GOD.....................184

Lesson EIGHT FAITH—THE REST OF GOD

I. INTRODUCTION

Faith is of vital importance to every believer. The New Testament states plainly that only faith will get a person born again into God's kingdom (Ephesians 2:8). Only by faith can an unbeliever appropriate the righteousness which God has made available (Philippians 3:9; Romans 3:28). But even after a person has exercised faith to be born again, he still needs to walk by faith. "As you therefore have received Christ Jesus the Lord, so walk in Him, having been firmly rooted and now being built up in Him and established in your faith . . ."(Colossians 2:6, 7) you received the Lord by faith, and now you are to walk by faith.

The importance of faith can be seen in the fact that it is impossible to please God without it "And without faith, it is impossible to please Him; for he who comes to God must believe that He is, and that He is a rewarder of those who seek Him" (Hebrews 11:6). God is pleased with faith, for faith is the way in which we receive what He has provided for us. Those who come to God must make two judgments about Him. One must believe that God is. This is a judgment about God's existence and about His power (Romans 1:20). One must believe that God is a rewarder of those who seek Him. This is a judgment about God's character. So in order to please God, we must have faith; and faith is our conviction not only of God's power and ability, but also of His willingness to use that power and ability in our behalf.

II. RECEIVING THE PROMISES OF GOD

Through Christ's atoning work on the cross, God has given to us all things which pertain to life and godliness (II Peter 1:3). His death has provided for us redemption and salvation, both spiritually and physically Through Jesus, total provision has been made for any need we might encounter in this life. The Word of God is full of God's promises to His children, and "all the promises of God in Him are yea, and in Him Amen, unto the glory of God by us" (II Corinthians 1:20).

But while all this is available to the Christian, these promised blessings from God will not come automatically. There is a part which each person must play in receiving what God has provided. God promised the land of Canaan to the children of Israel, but He didn't magically transport them there out of Egypt. The children of Israel didn't wake up one morning to find themselves in the Promised Land. They had to go in and possess the land which the Lord God had already promised and given. In much the same way, many believers need to go in and possess what God has already promised and provided for them through the Lord Jesus. God has done His part and now waits for His children to do their part. He waits for His children to exercise FAITH in what He has already done, and so receive and posses the provision that He has made for them.

A. REDEEMED FROM THE CURSE OF THE LAW

Perhaps the best statement as to the scope of our redemption is found in the book of Galatians. "Christ redeemed us from the curse of the Law, having become a curse for us—for it is written, 'Cursed is everyone that hangs on a tree'—in order that in Christ Jesus the blessing of Abraham might Come to the Gentiles, so that we might receive the promise of the Spirit through faith" (Galatians 3:13, 14).

1. The all-inclusive redemption
The curse of the Law mentioned here is listed in great detail in Deuteronomy chapter 28. That list sums up all that will happen to a person who sins by disobeying the laws of God. It includes sickness and disease (Deuteronomy 28:60, 61), financial poverty (Deuteronomy 28:38, 39), natural disaster (Deuteronomy 28:23, 24), and political turmoil (Deuteronomy 28:49-52).

All these calamities listed are things from which Christ, by His sacrifice, has redeemed us. Every believer has been redeemed from the curse of the Law, the curse that followed being a sinful creature. Sin has had devastating effects upon creation, but Christ's sacrifice has redeemed us from those Effects.

So Christ's redemption has not only purchased our release from sin, but also a release from the calamitous effects of sin. God's salvation is all-inclusive, taking in our whole spiritual, mental, and physical being. "He who did not spare His own Son, but delivered Him up for us all, how will He not also with Him, freely give us **ALL THINGS**" (Romans 8:32).

2. in this life

Yet to many believers, these great and precious promises are little more than a far away "promised land," never to be realized in this life. Some have relegated all these blessings to heaven or the millennial kingdom. But, these promises of God are meant to be enjoyed by believers in this life! The reason so many do not obtain them is because they fail to possess them. Like the Promised Land to the children of Israel, the provisions of the New Covenant are already granted; the price has already been paid. But, just like the land of Canaan to the Israelites, these provisions must be appropriated into the life of every individual believer.

B. PARTAKING OF OUR REDEMPTION

Study of the atoning work of Christ will show how broad and far-reaching our redemption really is. The promises of God, given to us in the Word, tell of a vast reservoir of blessing, healing, and deliverance at the disposal of every believer. But, it is up to the individual believer to "tap" into that vast reservoir for himself. He must possess what God has promised and provided.

The possession of God's promises and provisions are accomplished when a person exercises faith in God and in His Word. Faith is the spiritual quality which "taps" into God's reservoir and receives the promises of God. All the power of God and of His Word is available to anyone who will believe. But, unless faith is exercised, that power will never be realized.

1. Plugging into the power source

A simple but effective illustration of this principle can be seen in the rules which govern electricity and its use. All the electrical power necessary to operate an appliance is present in any electrical outlet. But, no matter how close to that outlet the appliance may be placed, no electricity will flow into it unless it is plugged in. One can place the appliance within inches of the outlet, for long periods of time, but nothing will happen.

The Appliance will only receive the electrical power that is in that outlet when it is plugged in and thus connected to the source of power.

In the same way, the only way anyone will ever receive from God's power source is to "plug in." Faith is the "plug" which will allow a person to tap the reservoir of God's power and receive the provision which He has made available. Just going to church for long periods of time will have no effect on a person if he never-uses faith to receive from God. Having hands laid on day after day will accomplish nothing for a person unless he exercises faith.

He will be just like that appliance which is set within inches of the outlet, but never plugged in. Not until he plugs into God's provision with his faith will that person possess what God has provided for him.

2. The touch of faith

Read Mark 5:21-34

Jesus had within Himself the power of God to heal the sick. He would lay His hands on the sick to allow that power to be transferred from Himself to the sick person. In this particular instance, however, there were numerous people touching Jesus. In fact, they were crowding in on Him as He walked to Jairus' house (Mark 5:24). Many people were in physical contact with Jesus at that moment, so His disciples were perplexed at His inquiry as to who had "touched" Him (Mark 5:30, 31).

But even though all those people were in physical contact with Jesus, only one had the power of God flow into her body. That was the woman who touched Jesus in faith. It was when someone touched Him in faith that Jesus knew that power had gone out of Him (Mark 5:30). Jesus commended the woman for her faith (Mark 5:34), stating that her faith had made her well. She was healed because her faith plugged into God's healing power and received what was necessary to drive that disease from her body and restore her to health.

It is plain to see from this passage that it is the touch of faith that releases God's power. When a person has faith in God and His Word, he begins to appropriate all the blessings which God has purchased for him. But unless that person exercises faith, he'll be like all the rest of the crowd that was pressing in on Jesus. They were right next to Him but did not experience the flow of God's power.

3. Failing to possess

The promise of God given to the children of Israel was that the land of Canaan belonged to them. All of God's power was at their disposal to enable them to possess what God had given them. Yet that particular generation never possessed God's provision for them because they would not believe the Word of God. They would not plug into God's power by faith.

"For we also have had the gospel preached to us, just as they did; but the message they heard was of no value to them, because those who heard did not combine it with faith," (Hebrews 4:2 NW),the message that the children of Israel heard was that the land was theirs, (Genesis 28:13, 14; 50:24); God's Angel would go before them to drive out the inhabitants (Exodus 23:23); God would cause all their enemies to turn and run from them (Exodus 23:27, 28).

In fact, it was known among the heathen Canaanite nations that God had given them the land, and so they were Terrified of the Israelites (Joshua 2:9).

And yet all the power of God, which was available to the children of Israel through God's Word, was of no avail to them because they would not "plug in" by faith. They didn't experience the blessings of God which belonged to them because of their unbelief, or lack of faith.

C. RELEASING THE POWER OF GOD

These few examples are sufficient to show that it is **FAITH** in God and His Word that will enable us to possess fully all the blessings of our redemption. Christ has redeemed us from all the curse of the Law and has made available to us all the blessings of our father, Abraham. Abraham's blessings were both spiritual and physical. Abraham was spiritually blessed because he had a relationship with Almighty God (Genesis 17:7). But, Abraham was also materially blessed (Genesis 13:2) and physically blessed in his body, being able to sire a son at the age of one hundred years (Genesis 21:5).

All these things belong to us, but we must appropriate them. It is the touch of faith that will release these things in our lives. It was faith that released the power of God into the woman's body. It was faith that enabled Caleb and 'Joshua to go into the Promised Land (Numbers 14:6-9; 32:11, 12). So too, it is faith that enables us to possess all that Christ has purchased for us in His great redemptive work on the cross.

Faith is the spiritual quality which connects us to the power of God. The Bible defines faith in the following way: "Now faith is the assurance (the confirmation, the title-deed) of things (we) hope for, being the proof of things (we) do not see and the conviction of their reality—faith perceiving as real fact what is not revealed to the senses" (Hebrews 11:1 Amplified).

Faith is an assurance of the heart. "For with the heart man believes . . ."(Romans 10:10). It is much more than a mere mental assent to certain information. It is a conviction of an unseen, spiritual reality. The promises of God are an unchanging, spiritual reality, whether they are being experienced in the "life of a believer or not. Faith perceives and is assured of the reality of these promises in the face of physical evidence to the contrary.

A. GOD'S UNSEEN REALITY

Inherent in the definition of faith given in Hebrews 11:1, and indeed in any discussion of the subject of faith, is the concept of an unseen reality. Faith is understood as a conviction of "things" which are not experienced by the physical senses. To walk by faith, then, means to walk with one's attention fixed on what is not seen rather than on what is seen. "While we look not at the things which are seen, but at the things which are not seen; for the things which are seen are temporal, but the things which are not seen are eternal" (II Corinthians 4:18).

Christians are called upon to "walk by faith and not by sight" (II Corinthians 5:7). This does not mean that we are to walk blind or in ignorance. It means rather that we are to fix our gaze on the unseen reality, the higher spiritual reality. The Bible says that the whole physical world that we see around us came into being out of the spiritual world which is physically "unseen" (Hebrews 11:3). So, the unseen spiritual reality of God is one which overrides and supercedes the seen physical reality which our senses experience.

1. The unseen spiritual realm

There exists around us an unseen spiritual realm. It is the realm in which God lives and operates. It is the realm in which angels work and in which demons live. Though it is not physically seen, it is nonetheless very real. This is the realm out of which God created the physical world in which we live. In fact, the whole physical world is predicated upon and has its source in the spiritual realm. This principle of an unseen realm is remarkably illustrated in II Kings 6:8-17. (Read this passage before proceeding.)

The Aramean (Syrian) king surrounded the city with a mighty army. In the physical realm, things looked rather grim. But, Elisha was aware of a higher reality. He was aware of the presence of an unseen host. The servant had to have his "eyes" opened to perceive it. Elisha's awareness of that unseen reality caused him to have great assurance about the outcome of the Aramean attack. He had confidence because he knew the spiritual reality outweighed the physical reality which his physical eyes were beholding.

2. Walking by the superior reality

"For we walk by faith, not by sight" (II Corinthians 5:7). We are to walk by faith, and not by sight, because we daily confront situations in which the reality we "see" does not correspond with the unseen reality God has given us "all things." When this occurs, our conviction and assurance must be fixed upon that unseen reality, as was Elisha's, and not upon physical circumstances. This is not to say that physical circumstances are illusionary. (That is what Christian Science teaches.) Physical circumstances are real, just as that Aramean army was real. But there is a higher principle of reality, which supercedes what our eyes see. That is the spiritual reality which Paul says we are to look to (II Corinthians 4:18).

3. Temporal vs. eternal reality

The things in the spiritual realm, which are unseen, are eternal; they never pass away. This cannot be said of this physical world. It is passing away. The things which are seen are "temporal"; they are subject to change. But the things which are unseen, those spiritual realities, are eternal; they will never change. Thus, it is easy to see why we should fix our confidence and assurance on the unseen things. Those are the things which remain.

If one only puts confidence on what he can see, he is destined to fail, and not become a partaker of the marvelous things which God has purchased for him. But if a person will put his trust and confidence in God's unseen realities, he'll begin to experience those blessings in his own life.

4. Abraham's assurance

Abraham was a man who was confronted with just such a contradiction. The physical circumstances said to Abraham that he and his wife, Sarah, could never have a son. He was 100 years old and she was 90. Yet God had spoken to them that they would bear a son. Abraham had a choice. He could believe what his body told him, or he could believe what God's Word said. He could walk by sight, or he could walk by faith.

Abraham chose to walk by faith, and so received from God a son in his old age. He was convinced of the reality and truth of God's Word, even though it was contradicted by what he could see. Abraham was assured that the unseen reality of God's Word was more real than what he could perceive with his physical senses (Romans 4:17-21).

B. GOD'S WORD REVEALS THE UNSEEN

Our "window" into this unseen reality is the Word of God. It is God's Word which informs us of the fact that we are more than conquerors (Romans 8:37). It is the Word which tells us that we were healed by the wounds of Jesus (I Peter 2:24) God's Word gives us insight into our son ship through the Lord Jesus (I John 3:1). Without the Bible, our perception would be limited to what our senses could tell us. But with the Bible, we can receive information which is 'truer than what we perceive in the physical world.

1. Revelation knowledge

The Word of God will "open our eyes" in much the same way as Elisha's servant had his "eyes" opened. This doesn't refer to physical vision. It speaks of revelation knowledge given by the Holy Spirit, which enables us to see the way things really are.

"Now we have received, not the spirit of the world, but the Spirit who is from God, that we might know the things freely given to us by God" (I Corinthians 2:12). The Spirit of God will show us all that belongs to us by opening the Word to us (John 14:26). As we said, the Word describes reality, because 'it informs us of all that is ours in Jesus Christ. God has already given to us all things which pertain to life and godliness. As the Spirit unfolds to us from the scriptures what these "things" are, we will become more and more convinced of their reality in the face of seeming contradiction.

2. Spiritual perception

Walking by faith is walking by the Word. It is basing our judgments not upon what we see, but upon what the Bible says. If our body says we are sick, but the Word says that we were healed, then we must base our judgment of reality on the Word. We are healed! If we feel rejected, but the Bible says that God loves and accepts us, our conviction must rest with the Word. We are loved and accepted by God! To live by the Word, and base our judgments upon it, we must know what the scriptures say. Ignorance of the Bible keeps people in bondage, because it keeps them blind to the reality of what God has done for them. Paul's prayer for the churches was that they might know.

"We have not Ceased to pray for you and to ask that you may be filled with the knowledge of His will in all spiritual wisdom and understanding" (Colossians 1:9). "I pray that the eyes of your heart may be enlightened, so that you may know . . ."(Ephesians1:18).

Paul was praying for their spiritual perception in much the same way as Elisha prayed for his servant. God's Word is what will give to us that perception of the unseen realm in which God lives, and in which He has given to us all the blessings and provisions of our redemption. The clearer our perception of those unseen realities, the more we will experience them in our lives.

C. FAITH THAT PLEASES GOD

A believer pleases God when he puts his confidence in the truth of God's Word, and is assured of a reality which he cannot see. This kind of person believes before he sees any result in the seen realm. A faithless person insists on physical evidence before he will believe. This kind of person will not believe in healing until he sees physical proof of recovery. He will not believe that God supplies all his needs unless his bank account is full. He does not please God, because he will never receive the blessings which God has given to him.

1. The problem of Thomas—faithlessness

Read John 20:24-29

Thomas made a statement which many are still making today. "Unless I shall see in His hands the imprint of the nails, and put my finger into the place of the nails, and put my hand into His side, I Will not believe" (John 20:25). Today's version is a little modified, but in essence, still the same—"Seeing is believing!" Jesus rebuked Thomas for his faithlessness because he wouldn't believe until he saw something with his own eyes. The promise of God and the Word of Jesus were not good enough for him. Jesus called this kind of attitude, one which demands physical proof before being convinced, faithlessness!

But, Jesus pronounced a blessing upon those who would believe, having not yet seen. "Because you have seen me, have you believed? Blessed are they who did not see, and yet believed" (John 20:29). This is the kind of faith that pleases God. God is looking for people who will take Him at His Word and believe without having any physical evidence to prove the reality of what He has said.

D. POSSESSING GOD'S PROMISES THROUGH FAITH

Through the death of Jesus, God has given to us many great and precious promises. These promises sum up all that our redemption entails for us. But as we have said, the promises of God don't automatically fall on believers. They must be received or possessed, in much the same way in which the Israelites had to possess the promised land of Canaan. The promises of God are received by faith. Faith is the factor which activates the power of God and brings those promises into physical reality in our lives.

Faith connects us to God's provision, because faith is our assurance of that provision while it is yet unseen. Our assurance must be fixed firmly on the truth of God's Word, and on the reality that the provision has already been granted through the Lord Jesus. All the promises of God are yes! And Amen! in Jesus, because Jesus has already paid the price for them.

1. Wondering & wishing

Wondering why one doesn't receive, or wishing that one would receive, won't release God's power to bring about an answer. Wondering and wishing are not the ways to possess the inheritance. Those who wish they had the provision sincerely desire it, but are convinced that they do not yet have it. They only believe what they can perceive with their five physical senses. "Faith perceives as real fact what is not revealed to the senses" (Hebrews 11:1 Amplified). Before anyone can begin to experience the provision which redemption has given, he must begin to see as real fact what he does not yet see in physical manifestation. He must begin to see as real fact that he is healed, even though his body may be sick.

He must be assured that all his needs are met, even though his bank account may be empty. This assurance of the reality of the unseen, as it is revealed in God's Word, is the thing that will bring into manifestation all the blessings of God's redemptive inheritance.

2. Bible faith

Jesus Himself taught this very principle of faith to His disciples. After telling them to have faith in God, He went on to say, "Therefore I tell you, whatever you ask for in prayer, believe that you have received it, and it will be yours" (Mark 11:24 NW). The principle given here is clear. Believe that you have received (past tense) before you see anything, and then it will be yours.

This is Biblical faith, the faith which appropriates the blessings of God. We must believe that the promises and provisions of God, as they are shown in the scriptures, are already ours before we will experience them. Faith is our assurance and conviction that we have them even though we do not yet see them.

IV. FAITH—A POSITION OF REST

Faith that pleases God is that which believes that God is a rewarder of those who seek Him (Hebrews 11:6). To stand in the assurance of faith, one must be assured that God is a liberal giver (James 1:5) and not a withholder (Psalm 84:11). Thus, one can see that faith is not a struggle with God to try to get Him to move in our behalf. God already has moved in our behalf, by giving to us all things that pertain to life and godliness.

Faith is not even a struggle to try to overcome difficulties by our own power or ability, "for the battle is not yours, but God's" (II Chronicles 20:15).

Faith is a position of rest, a confident assurance of what God has already done for us, and a conviction that it will come to pass in our own experience. When we believe, we enter into rest, because faith sees things from God's perspective—the way things really are. Thus, the walk of faith to which we have been called is one of rest, not of struggle and strain. Jesus said, "Come unto Me, all who are weary and heavy—laden, and I will give you rest. Take my yoke upon you, and learn from me, for I am gentle and humble in heart; and you shall find rest for your souls. For My yoke is easy (pleasant), and my load is light" (Matthew 11:28-30).

A. REVELATION OF GOD'S LOVE

Paul prayed for the Ephesian believers, that they would come to a full knowledge of the love of God (Ephesians 3:17-19). Many times, believers have trouble with faith because they have a very vague understanding of God's love and mercy. The enemy has portrayed God to them as an angry ogre, who will not give anything to them until a list of criteria has been met. In the eyes of these Christians, God is not a rewarder, but a withholder. Faith to them is a formula, which must be followed to the letter before God will move.

This type of thinking exposes a fundamental misunderstanding about the nature of God. In Lesson 2, we established what the Bible says about God's character. God is Love (I John 4:16). He doesn't just have love; He IS love! God is not a demanding task-master who is waiting for His "servants" to "toe the line."

God is a loving Father who longs to reward His children, and bestow "good and perfect gifts" upon them (James 1:17). So much did He love us, that He sent His Son to redeem us from sin and to give us "all things" (I Corinthians 3:21-23).

1. Faith responds to grace
Faith is our heart's response to the unmerited favor of God, as it is revealed in His Word. The Bible tells how much God loves us, by showing all that

He has done for us through the death of His Son. When a person spends time meditating on the revelation of God's love, as it is shown in the Word, and begins to comprehend the love of God "which surpasses knowledge," his heart will respond with faith. It was God's grace (unmerited favor) that caused us to be born again. "For by grace you have been saved through faith;" (Ephesians 2:8). The unmerited favor of God is what caused Him to sacrifice His only Son. Faith is simply our response to that gracious act. Thus, faith is not a "work" by which we can earn God's love. God's love and favor cannot be earned. Faith is our assurance of what God, by His grace, has freely given to us.

2. Having faith in God's faithfulness
The rest of faith is a confidence in God's love and faithfulness. God is faithful. It was because Sarah judged Him so, that she received strength to conceive Isaac in her old age (Hebrews 11:11). Resting in faith is resting in the unfailing goodness and mercy of God. "0 give thanks unto the Lord; for He is good; for His mercy endureth for ever" (Psalm 136:1 KJV).

B. FAITH IS OF THE SPIRIT

The assurance of faith, which enables a man to hold himself calm in the midst of adversity, is a supernatural phenomenon. Jesus often exhibited this kind of assurance during His earthly ministry. When a storm almost sank the boat in which He was traveling, His disciples were 'beside themselves with fear. But, Jesus remained calm (Mark 4:35-39). This kind of calm assurance arose out of His spirit. It is with the heart that a man believes (Romans 10:10), and that is where the rest of faith comes from.

Faith is of the spirit. It is not a mental phenomenon, neither is it an emotional phenomenon. Faith is a spiritual force which comes out of a man's heart. That spiritual force within will override any mental reservation or fears that a person may have if he will allow it to do so.

1. Faith is not intellectual (mental assent)
Faith is not of the mind. It is not a mental phenomenon. One must be careful not to confuse faith with mental assent. Mental assent superficially agrees with the Word of God, but when the pressure is on, it responds in much the same way as the disciples did during that storm. Mental assent

will not give a person the assurance as to the reality of what the Word says. It will always agree with circumstances rather than with the Word, whenever there is a discrepancy between the two.

2. Faith is not emotional excitement (feelings)

Faith is not of the emotions. It is not an emotional phenomenon. Often, well-meaning Christians will confuse emotional zeal with faith. Faith is a rest and assurance of the heart, not an excitement of the emotions. The assurance of faith will sometimes result in an emotional response, but if one has emotions with no real assurance to back it up, that emotional excitement will always wither in the face of contrary circumstances (Mark 4:16,17).

Peter, in a moment of great emotional excitement, said that he would never deny the Lord Jesus. Yet when the pressure was on, this is exactly what he did. He had no real faith to back up his zeal, and so his zeal withered in the face of adversity (Luke 22:33, 34, 60, 61). Yet later, when faced with another adverse situation, Peter had real faith to back up his zeal. He confidently looked at the Pharisees of the Sanhedrin and said, "We must obey God rather than men" (Acts 5:27-29).

"Behold, God is my salvation, I will trust and not be afraid; for the Lord God is my strength and song, and He has become my salvation" (Isaiah 12:2). Faith is a position of rest, because faith recognizes that salvation is from the Lord, and from nowhere else. Putting assurance in anything else (e.g. Intellectual ideas or emotional excitement) is bound to lead to disappointment. But, putting trust and assurance in the Living God will always result in our receiving from God what He-desires for us to receive. As we cease from our own efforts, and put our confidence in the goodness and faithfulness of God, we'll experience that rest of faith to which Jesus has called us, and receive from the bountifulness of God's hand.

V. SUMMARY—THE FAITH THAT PLEASES GOD

We must walk by faith in order to please God, believing that He is faithful and a rewarder of those who seek Him. This is the way in which we will experience all that God has purchased for us through His great salvation walking by faith means basing our judgments on what the Word of God says rather than on what physical circumstances say. We are to look to the unseen reality which the scriptures describe, and as we do, those unseen things will begin to be manifested in our experience. **Real Bible faith involves believing** that we have received before seeing physical proof. In this way, we will tap into all that God has purchased for us and so desires us to experience.

LESSON EIGHT
DAY ONE
FAITH—THE REST OF GOD STUDY QUESTIONS

1. According to Hebrews 11:6, those who come to God must believe two things. What are they, and what is the judgment that we make with each?

a. _____

b. _____

Our faith, then, is a conviction not only of God's ability, but also of

_____

2. How does (Galatians 3:13) sum up all that God has done for us on Calvary?

_____

_____

_____

3. How is the possession of God's promises and provisions accomplished?

_____

4. In your own words, explain how the rules which govern electricity and its use compare with the relation between faith and the power of God?

_____

_____

5. Why did an entire generation of Israelites fail to possess what God had promised them? (Give scriptures.) How does this apply to us today?

_____

_____

_____

LESSON EIGHT

DAY TWO

FAITH—THE REST OF GOD STUDY QUESTIONS

1. What does it mean to "walk by faith"?

   _____

   _____

2. Give three examples of people from the Bible who were assured of the greater spiritual reality, in the face of seeming physical contradiction. Explain the contradiction which each one faced, and how each one responded to it.

   a. _____

   _____

   _____

   b. _____

   _____

   _____

   c. _____

   _____

3. Explain this statement: "The Word of God 'opens our eyes.' "What does it mean to have our "eyes" opened? How are they opened?

   _____

   _____

   _____

   _____

4. Have you ever had your "eyes" opened? Tell how this happened, and what it was that you perceived about God and His Word.

   _____

   _____

   _____

   _____

LESSON EIGHT

DAY THREE

FAITH—THE REST OF GOD STUDY QUESTIONS

1. How does ignorance of the spiritual realities which are revealed in God's Word keep Christians in bondage?

_____

_____

_____

_____

_____

2. Read II Chronicles 20:1-25. Explain how King Jehoshaphat and his people operated in faith when faced with adversity. What was their response to the Word of the Lord? How did they demonstrate their convictions? What was the result of their faith and trust in the Lord?

_____

_____

_____

_____

_____

3. In what ways will you apply the lessons to be learned from Jehoshaphat's example to your own life?

_____

_____

_____

_____

_____

LESSON EIGHT
DAY FOUR
FAITH—THE REST OF GOD STUDY QUESTIONS

1. Faith is not a _____, but a position of _____!

   Many Christians have trouble with faith because they don't fully understand the love of God. What is the relationship between our knowledge of God's love and our faith? Why is faith merely a formula to those who don't see the love of God?

   _____

   _____

   _____

   _____

3. What is the difference between faith and "mental assent"?

   _____

   _____

   _____

   _____

4. What is the difference between faith and "emotional zeal"?

   _____

   _____

   _____

5. Give an example from your own life in which you had to stand in faith with only the Bible as proof or evidence that you possessed what God had given you.

   _____

   _____

   _____

   _____

Lesson NINE FAITH'S CONFESSION: THE EXAMPLE OF GOD

Lesson NINE FAITH'S CONFESSION:
THE EXAMPLE OF GOD

I. INTRODUCTION 195

II. OUR MEASURE OF FAITH..195
    A. Faith Comes by Hearing 196
        1. Knowing the revealed will of God
        2. Examples
    B. Faith Can be Developed 197
        1. Continue in the Word
        2. Exercise
        3. The growth process

III. ACTING ON THE WORD 199
    A. Faith and Obedience...200
        1. The sick friend—Luke 5:17-20
        2. The ten lepers—Luke 17:11-14
        3. Peter walks on water—Matthew 14:25-32
    B. What It Means to be a Doer of the Word................................201
        1. Proper foundations and storms
        2. The assured heart

IV. FAITH'S CONFESSION 203
    A. The God-Kind of Faith...204
        1. Abraham's name change
        2. How it works
    B. Confession Brings Possession...205
        1. Jesus and the centurion
        2. Address the mountain
    C. Speak Your Faith..207
        1. Guard your speech
        2. The power of the tongue
        3. The heart & mouth connection

V. SUMMARY—FAITH THAT SPEAKS 209

Lesson NINE FAITH'S CONFESSION: THE EXAMPLE OF GOD

I. INTRODUCTION

In the previous lesson we saw that it is by faith we receive all that God has given to us. God's only means of getting to us all that He has accomplished in Christ is through faith. That is why there is no more important theme in the New Testament. God's desire is that His children develop their faith, so that they can walk in it more and more each day.

God is much like our earthly parents in that He desires our development and growth. Just as parents are ecstatic about their child's first word or step, so God is pleased about our faith in His Word. He longs to see His children mature in the area of faith, so that they are able to stand on their own feet.

God has given to every Christian the same ability and potential for growth. Those who are strong in faith are not so because they are God's "favorites"; "God is not one to show partiality" (Acts 10:34). They are strong in faith because they have developed their faith through God's Word. Every believer has been given this same opportunity for spiritual development, and so every believer is capable of having strong faith.

II. OUR MEASURE OF FAITH

Any person who is born again has faith enough to appropriate God's righteousness. Thus, every Christian has faith. If a Christian did not have faith, he would not be saved. "For by grace you have been saved through faith" (Ephesians 2:8). Often, the enemy will put believers under condemnation by telling them that they don't have any faith. But,

THE Bible states that every child of God has faith, "For through the grace given to me I say to every Man among you not to think more highly of himself than he ought to think; but to think so as to Have sound judgment, as God has allotted to each a measure of faith" (Romans 12:3).

God is a just God and would not require anything of His children which they were not able to do. God always gives us the ability to do what He commands before giving us the command. God is looking for us to live

195

and to walk by faith. But He has also given to us the ability to do this, because He has allotted to each of us a measure of faith. This faith comes by the Word of God, and can be developed. It is up to the individual believer as to whether or not he will begin to exercise that faith which God has given to him, and develop it through the Word.

A. FAITH COMES BY HEARING

God's means of giving us faith, and increasing that faith, is His Word. "So faith comes from hearing, and hearing by the word of Christ" (Romans 10:17). The Word of God is what gives rise to faith in our spirits. Here we have a simple way in which we can obtain faith for any area of our lives. Faith will come as we read and meditate on the scriptures. We don't need to work it up, or strain to get it; faith comes automatically as we partake of God's Word.

1. Knowing the revealed will of God

Faith rests upon the revealed will of God. Only when you know the will of God in a matter can you have faith in that area. If you don't know that it is God's will to save, then you can't have faith for Salvation. If you don't know that it is God's will to heal, then you can't have faith for healing. If you don't know that it is God's will to bless, then you can't have faith to be blessed of God. The Bible reveals to us what God's will is by showing us all that God has already done through His Son. The Word reveals His will for salvation by showing how it was purchased for all on Calvary (I John 2:2), and stating that "Whoever will call upon the name of the Lord will be saved" (Romans 10:13). We know the will of God in the area of healing, because the Bible states that Jesus paid the price for it on the cross (Matthew 8:17). Faith arises in one's heart when he begins to see what God's will for him really is, and that the price to bring that will to pass has already been paid in full.

2. Examples

Faith comes by hearing the revealed will of God, which is found in His Word. Paul once preached the gospel (Word of God) in a town called Lystra and in the crowd was a lame man. "This man was listening to Paul as he spoke, who, when he had fixed his gaze upon him, and had seen that he had faith to be made well, said with a loud voice, 'Stand upright on your feet.' And he leaped up and began to walk." (Acts 14:9—10) The man obtained faith to be healed because he heard the Word preached, and faith sprang up in his heart. The hearing of the Word produced faith, and faith brought about the lame man's deliverance. Much the same thing happened to Cornelius the centurion. Without so much as an altar call, Cornelius and his entire family were saved and filled with the Holy Spirit. He had been told by an angel to send for Peter, who would speak words by which he and his entire household would be saved. (Acts 11:13, 14) As Peter preached the Word to them the Holy Spirit fell upon them. Since the Spirit is only poured out on believers, it is safe to assume that Cornelius believed and was saved while he was hearing the Word of God from the mouth of the apostle Peter (Read Acts, chapter 10).

In both these examples from the scriptures, it is obvious that the faith which these men exhibited came as a result of their hearing the good news. Faith for any of God's blessings comes as a person hears the Word which declares those blessings to be God's will for all men.

B. FAITH CAN BE DEVELOPED

It is evident from the scriptures that faith is a measurable Spiritual quality Jesus spoke of those who had no faith (Mark 4:40), those who had little faith (Matthew 14:31); 16:8); and those who had great faith (Matthew 8:10; 15:28).

The Bible has many references to different types and stages of faith.

- Romans 4:19, 20 Weak and strong faith compared

- James 2:5 Rich in faith

- Acts 6:5 Full of faith

- James 2:22 Perfect faith

- I Timothy 1:5 Unfeigned faith

- I John 5:4 Overcoming faith

- I Timothy 1:19 Shipwrecked faith

Not only is faith measurable, but it can be increased and developed. It is possible, if not essential, for a Christian to grow in faith. "We ought always to thank God for you, brothers, and rightly so, because your faith is growing more and more" (II Thessalonians 1:3 NW).

This type of growth in faith is available to every Christian, not just to a select few "faith giants." God wants all of His children to be men and women of great faith, and not those of "little faith." He has put at our disposal all the tools and instructions necessary for us to grow in faith. If we will use them, we too will have a faith that is "growing more and more."

1. Continue in the Word

Just as faith comes through the Word of God, so faith also grows as we feed on and meditate in His Word. It is not enough just to hear the Word once, and then assume that no more hearing of the Word is necessary. No one will ever grow in faith unless he continues in the Word. Faith will wither and die when one is not fed with the Word, just as a plant will die if it is not watered. In order to grow in faith, one must constantly reaffirm in his heart and mind the truth of what God has spoken.

Faith grows in an atmosphere where the Word of God is constantly going forth. This means at home, in one's own personal study time, and at a church where the Word is being preached. It is impossible for faith to grow when one hears the Word only intermittently, or when one constantly hears teaching that is contrary to faith. Faith for healing will not develop in a place where sickness is preached as the will of God. Faith for prosperity will not grow where poverty is taught as a virtue. Faith will only grow when a person consistently subjects himself to hearing the Word, at a church where it is taught, and at home in personal study.

2. Exercise

Exercise is another factor necessary for growing faith. Faith grows when it is used just as muscles develop when they are worked, so too, our faith develops when we use it. The disciples once asked Jesus to increase their faith. Jesus responded, "If you had faith like a mustard seed, you would say to this mulberry tree, 'Be uprooted and be planted in the sea'; and it would obey you" (Luke 17:6). Jesus' answer to their request for increased faith was simply an exhortation to use what they already had.

Faith will increase when it is used. Every time we stand in faith for the blessings of God, we are becoming stronger and stronger in that faith. Faith will not develop if it is not used, any more than muscles will develop if they are not used. To grow in faith, we must use the faith that we already have by standing and acting on the Word.

3. The growth process

Growth and development don't occur overnight. It takes time to increase faith—time to hear and meditate in the Word, and time to exercise the faith that one has. Christians are not born again with the faith to move Mt. Everest! Trying to believe God for something that is beyond your maturity in faith will only lead to discouragement. For example, it is absurd to believe God for a new car, when one has never even believed God for a new pair of shoes. Faith grows a step at a time, not in one gigantic leap.

It is essential that Christians avoid making comparisons between themselves and other believers. Too often people try to emulate men of faith without realizing all that has gone into their growth. They want to be able to believe God for the same mighty things they see others receiving, without taking the time to hear the Word and develop their own faith.

If a man is strong in faith, one can be assured that he didn't get that way in a day. Strong faith is a result of spending time consistently hearing and meditating in the Word, and then exercising that faith until it becomes strong and vibrant.

III. ACTING ON THE WORD

Faith is "the assurance of things hoped for, the conviction of things not seen" (Hebrews 11:1). Faith is an inward assurance and conviction; it is with the heart that a man believes (Romans 10:10). That assurance of the heart will always make itself known in action. If a person says that he has that inner assurance, yet shows no outward actions to prove it, then he is self-deluded. The apostle James said that faith without works is dead, or useless (James 2:17, 20, 26). In other words, faith without corresponding actions is not the Faith without works is really nothing more than mental assent. Mental assent is an agreement with the Word of God which has no action to back it up. Often, mental assent will appear to be very much like real faith. But the discriminating factor between the two is action.

The "believer" will always act on his convictions, while the "mental assenter" will never show any corresponding actions to what he "agrees" is true."But prove yourselves doers of the Word, and not merely hearers who delude themselves" (James 1:22). Walking by faith in the Word of God means being a doer of the Word. It means acting in accordance with the assurance that is within our hearts. Now works or actions done without that inward assurance are not faith. But Bible faith must always have corresponding actions which give evidence of that inward conviction of the heart. It was when Abraham acted on what he believed that his faith was perfected (James 2:22), and he received from God.

A. FAITH AND OBEDIENCE

"By faith Abraham, when he was called, obeyed by going out to a place which he was to receive for an inheritance; and he went out, not knowing where he was going" (Hebrews 11:8). Abraham's obedience sprang out of the assurance that was in his heart. He left his home to receive the promise of God which he had never seen, because he was convinced of the truthfulness and reality of that promise. Out of this conviction came action.

If Abraham had never acted in obedience to God's call, all his "faith" in God's promise would have been totally useless, or dead. It wasn't Abraham's mental assent to the promise of God that enabled him to receive. It was his obedience that brought about the fulfillment of the promise. If he hadn't acted on his conviction, his faith would have been dead, and he never would have become the "father of many nations."

Several times during the earthly ministry of Jesus, people received a miracle as they acted in correspondence with their faith. The actions they displayed were a witness of the faith that was in their hearts. We will look at three such incidents.

1. The sick friend—Luke 5:17-20
Jesus recognized faith in men's actions. Four men once cut a hole in the roof of the house in which Jesus was teaching in order to lower their sick friend into His presence. They couldn't get him through the door because of the crowd. As they lowered the sick man in front of Jesus, the Bible says that Jesus "saw their faith" (Luke 5:20). In that act, He recognized the real inward assurance of their hearts. (Read Luke 5:17-20.) So assured

were they that God's power would deliver their oppressed friend, that nothing would discourage them from getting him to Jesus.

2. The ten lepers—Luke 17:11-14

When ten lepers cried out to Jesus for mercy, He simply instructed them to go and show themselves to the priest. Under Levitical law, when a leper had received deliverance from the disease, then he was to go to the priest and make the proper sacrifices (Leviticus 14:1-4). Jesus told these men to go before they had received any manifestation of cleansing. "And it came about that as they were going, they were cleansed" (Luke 17:14). They received a miracle when they acted in obedience to the Word of Jesus. Their action was a demonstration of their conviction of God's power to heal.

3. Peter walks on water—Matthew 14:25-32

In the account of Jesus and Peter walking on the water, attention is usually focused on Peter's failure. But here we will focus on the fact that Peter did indeed walk on the water. Jesus told Peter to come, and Peter acted on that command. The other eleven disciples didn't walk on water like Peter, because they didn't get out of the boat. Their "faith" was useless and accomplished nothing in that situation because they did not act. But Peter did act, and although he feared and began to sink, the fact remains that he walked on water. The rest of the disciples just sat in the boat looking. They didn't receive a miracle because they added no action to their faith. If you want to walk on water, you have to get out of the boat.

B. WHAT IT MEANS TO BE A DOER OF THE WORD

If a person is not a doer of the Word, but simply one who hears and doesn't act, the Bible says that he is self-deluded (James 1:22). This delusion arises when a person fails to distinguish between faith and mental assent. Faith and mental assent are in many ways similar. Both hear the Word of God. Both rejoice over the Word. Both state with conviction that they believe the Bible. But the difference between the two is shown in their works. Faith always has actions corresponding to an inward assurance. Mental assent never has any action attached to it. The one who hears but doesn't act is deluded into thinking that he has faith, when in reality he is simply mentally assenting to the Word.

1. Proper foundations and storms

Jesus Himself called upon men to be doers of the Word. He likened the doer to a wise man who built his house with foundations on the rock. When the storms came, the house stood. The hearer of the Word was likened to a fool who laid no foundation for his house at all. When the storm came, his house fell (Luke 6:46-49). Notice that before the storm, the wise man and the fool fared the same. But when the storm arrived, the difference between the two quickly became apparent.

To hear the Word and not act on it is as foolish as building a house without a foundation. The house won't last, and neither will the person who only hears. It is the doer of the Word, the one who acts on the conviction in his heart that will not be shaken. He will stand solidly in the midst of the storm, just like the house that is founded on the rock.

2. The assured heart

Faith comes by hearing (Romans 10:17). It is apparent from the scriptures that the first step in obtaining and developing faith is hearing the Word of God. That is the only way that we can get that settled assurance in our hearts. Then, when that conviction is settled within, we are to act on it. It is wrong, however, to act and step out when we don't have that inner assurance. Just stepping out and acting are not, in and of themselves, faith. Faith is not action; it is a condition of the heart.

"But the one who looks intently at the perfect law, the law of liberty, and abides by it, not having become a forgetful hearer but an effectual doer, this man shall be blessed in what he does" (James 1:25). One will not be an effectual doer until he has looked intently into the Word. Hearing has to come before acting. Some try to act when they haven't really yet heard, thinking that their action, in and of itself, is faith. But the works that please God are those that are done out of a heart that is fully assured of God's Word. These are the works which faith will manifest, and without which faith is dead.

It is the condition of the heart that pleases God, and not the works themselves. We cannot buy God's approval, or get Him to move in our behalf, by doing good works. Abraham was blessed because his heart was assured of God's goodness, not because of his works. The works which he did (i.e. his obedience to God) were simply indicative of what was already within his heart.

IV. FAITH'S CONFESSION

The word "confession" is often used only in a negative sense, denoting an admission of sin and guilt. This indeed is a scriptural usage of the word (I John 1:9), but by no means It's only meaning. More often when the Bible uses the word "confession," it is used in the positive sense of affirming ones faith with his mouth. Jesus is said to have had a good confession before Pontius Pilate (I Timothy 6:13), and this could not refer to an admission of sin. In the book of Hebrews, we are told to hold fast the confession of our hope (Hebrews 10:23). One of the basic principles of Christianity is the confession of faith. Down through the centuries this has degenerated into a ritual, in which some words are mouthed for gaining church membership. But, the confession that comes from our mouths is an integral part of any faith that we have.

Paul stated that a man is saved when he believes and speaks! "If you confess with your mouth Jesus as Lord, and believe in your heart that God raised Him from the dead, you shall be saved" (Romans 10:9). The word of faith is not just in our hearts; it must also be in our mouths. "The word is near you, in your mouth and in your heart'—that is, the word of faith which we are preaching" (Romans 10:8).

"But having the same spirit of faith, according to what is written, 'I believed, therefore I spoke,' we also believe, therefore we speak" (II Corinthians 4:13). The spirit of faith is one that believes and then speaks out that assurance which is in the heart. Faith always has a good confession which affirms the truth and reality of God's promises. This verbal affirmation of faith comes before there is any manifestation of the promise's fulfillment. Remember that faith believes that God has provided the answer before it sees the result. So also, confession is made of the reality of God's Word, even when the results have not yet been manifested in the seen realm.

A. THE GOD-KIND OF FAITH

God is a faith God and operates in this same spirit of faith. When He created the universe, He did so with His words. "By faith we understand that the worlds were prepared by the word of God" (Hebrews 11:3). In Genesis, chapter 1, we see that God said, "Let there be light!" (Genesis 1:3), and it was so. Jesus called this the faith of God (or the God-kind of faith). In teaching His disciples (and us) about faith, Jesus said. "Have faith in God (have the faith of God—marginal reading). For verily I say unto you, That whosoever shall say unto this mountain, Be thou removed, and be thou cast into the sea; and shall not doubt in his heart, but shall believe that those things which he saith shall come to pass; he shall have whatsoever he saith" (Mark 11:22,23 KJV). The God—kind of faith is faith that speaks what it believes. Notice that the word "say" appears more times in Jesus' lesson on faith than does the word "believe." We are to believe that what we say will come to pass. Many Christians think that what they believe will come to pass. But the word of faith is in our mouths, and must be spoken out if we are to receive from God.

1. Abraham's name change

God demonstrated this kind of faith in His dealings with His friend, Abram. God promised Abram a son, and then spoke His faith by changing Abram's name to Abraham. "Abraham" means "the father of a multitude." God called His friend "father of a multitude" before the promised son was even conceived. "No longer will you be called Abram, your name shall be Abraham; for I have made you a father of many nations" (Genesis 17:5 NW).

In the eyes of God, the promised son was an accomplished reality, so God spoke His faith by calling Abram a "father of a multitude," or Abraham. In the cultural setting of Abraham's day, a person's name had great significance; one's name described his characteristics, and in many ways stated who and what that person was. Every time Abraham introduced himself by his new name, he was in effect making a statement to whomever he met that he was at that moment the "father of a multitude," even though Isaac was as yet unborn. (Read Genesis, chapter 17).

2. How it works

This is the way in which the God-kind of faith works. It is in the very nature of God to speak of spiritual realities as though they already existed in the physical realm. In the book of Romans, Paul lists two great attributes of God. He refers to Him as "the God who gives life to the dead and calls those things that are not as though they were" (Romans 4:17 NW). That God is One who gives life to the dead, no one will dispute. But, it is just as much a part of His nature to call things which are not (in the physical realm) as though they already existed. This He demonstrated by renaming Abram, Abraham.

The God-kind of faith, then, is faith that speaks what it believes. Faith is not fully functional until a person is speaking from the assurance that is within his heart. When he does so, he is operating in the same spirit of faith in which God operates. He believes; therefore he speaks.

B. CONFESSION BRINGS POSSESSION

The positive confession of God's Word is an essential part of the faith which receives from God. It is as a person begins to speak out his faith in the Word of God that the "mountains" will begin to move. Words will cause the things which we desire to come to pass, when they are spoken out of the full assurance of faith. Since faith comes by hearing the Word of God, it is apparent that the word which we speak must be God's, and not just our own. God's Word has all of His authority and power backing it up, so that when it is spoken in faith, it comes to pass.

Words, in and of them selves, are ineffective in the spiritual world. It is only when words are connected with faith in the heart that they accomplish things. The man who has whatever he says, is the man who doesn't doubt in his heart, but believes that what he says will happen (Mark 11:23). Words spoken with no corresponding faith in the heart will not move the mountain. The seven sons of Sceva once tried to speak words of authority over a demon, but had no faith in their hearts (they didn't believe in Jesus). The Bible says that their words were completely ineffective (Acts 19:13-16).

But, words spoken out of a heart that is full of faith in God and His Word are effective and carry great authority. When a believer speaks God's Word with the conviction of its reality in his heart, it is as though God Himself were speaking. The results are the same—the mountain will move.

1. Jesus and the centurion

Jesus exemplified this kind of faith in His earthly ministry. When a storm arose which threatened to capsize His boat, he spoke to the wind and the waves to be still, and they obeyed Him (Mark 4:37-39). When Peter's mother-in-law was sick with a fever, Jesus rebuked the fever, and it left her (Luke 4:38, 39). Jesus' words carried authority, because He believed that what He said would come to pass.

The centurion who came to Jesus on behalf of his sick servant understood the power of words. When Jesus offered to come to his house to heal the servant, the centurion replied that all Jesus need do was speak the word! **"But just say the word** and my servant will be healed. For I too am a man under authority, with soldiers under me; and I say to this one, 'Go!' and he goes, and to another, 'Come!' and he comes, and to my slave, 'Do this!' and he does it" (Matthew 8:8,9).

Jesus marveled at his great faith. The centurion knew that because he was a man who had authority, his words were effective. He recognized the same thing in Jesus. Jesus' words carried power to heal, because they were backed by the power of heaven. His word was sufficient to affect a cure in the sick man.

2. Address the mountain

In the same way the Word of God, spoken from the mouth of a believer, has the authority of Heaven behind it. The mountain will move when the Word is spoken. Many people believe for the mountain to move, but they don't speak to it; many pray and ask God to move the mountain, but never address it themselves. Jesus told us to speak to the mountain in faith

In this situation, He didn't tell us to pray; He told us to SAY! Too often, Christians are praying when they should be saying. There is a time for prayer; but there is also a time to open our mouths and speak to the mountain, difficulty, or adverse situation and command it to be gone.

When we do this, we are walking in the footsteps of our Lord, and following the instructions and examples that He left us.

C. SPEAK YOUR FAITH

The God-kind of faith always speaks what it believes. That assurance within a man's heart will find expression in a positive confession of God's Word. Jesus said that what is in a man's heart in abundance will be manifested by what he says with his mouth (Matthew 12:34, 35). In other words, you can always locate a person by their speech. If a person's heart is full of faith, it will be evident by what he says. This positive confession is made before there is any manifestation of it in the physical. Remember that God called Abram, Abraham, before Isaac was born. God calls things which are not as though they were, before they are manifested. We are to believe that we have received things before we have them; we are also to say that we have received before we have them.

This is exactly opposite to the way the world operates, but it is exactly in line with the way God operates. The pattern is simple.

1. Guard your speech
The scriptures are full of admonitions for believers to guard their speech. "The one who guards his mouth preserves his life; the one who opens wide his lips come to ruin" (Proverbs 13:3). "He who guards his mouth and his tongue guards his soul from troubles" (Proverbs 21:23). These are just two among many references which warn against being careless with words. Also read Proverbs 10:19; 17:28; Ecclesiastes 5:2; James 1:19; 3:2).

It is possible for a believer to make statements which tend to negate the faith in their heart. Often, when believing God for a particular thing, Christians will speak only what their eyes can see and their emotions can feel. If they are believing for healing, but haven't yet received a manifestation, their speech will be all about how sick they are.

What they should rather say is: "By His stripes I was healed" (I Peter 2:24). They may believe for financial prosperity, but their words are always a complaint about how they don't have enough money. They should rather say: "My God shall supply all my needs . . ."(Philippians 4:19).

2. The power of the tongue

"Death and life are in the power of the tongue, and those who love it will eat its fruit" (Proverbs 18:21). Few have realized the full import of this statement. A person can experience life or death depending on what he allows to come forth from his mouth. Constant negative confession of doubt and despair will bring to pass those things which are being spoken. One negative statement said unwittingly or in jest, will not cause evil to come about. But if a believer gets into the habit of continually confessing negative things, he'll get to a point where his heart will start to believe the things which his mouth is continually saying. When the words of his mouth begin to align with what he believes in his heart, the principle of Mark 11:23 will be fulfilled in a negative sense.

One negative statement will not bring disaster on a believer. There are times when we must-inform those who can help us of what our problem is. Having a positive confession does not mean that we are to hide our difficulties from our brethren. The thing to be avoided is the continual confession of defeat. This is why we must put a guard on our mouths and not allow ourselves the luxury of an undisciplined mouth. The occasional negative confession will turn into the frequent negative confession, and the frequent negative confession will soon become a continual negative confession. Thus, it is best to stop negative statements while they are still occasional, rather than waiting until they are a deep-seated habit.

3. The heart & mouth connection

When a person is believing in God and exercising faith, he must maintain a positive confession of God's Word. It is the confession of the Word, when connected with assurance in one's heart that will bring about a manifestation of the answer. This confession must be made out of the conviction of one's heart. Remember that the one who does not doubt in his heart, but believes that what he says will come to pass, will have what he says. There must be a connection between the heart and the mouth. Thus; there are two purposes behind confessing God's Word. The first is so that we may become more and more assured in our hearts of what the Lord has to say about our situation.

A person confesses the Word aloud to himself; he is in reality meditating on the scriptures (remember, to meditate means "to mutter to oneself"). As he meditates on the Word by confessing again and again, the assurance of faith begins to rise up in his heart. Then he can speak to the mountain, fully believing God's Word on the subject, and the mountain will obey him. Just as the world is in the habit of saying things that are negative, so Christians can get into the habit of only speaking things which are in accordance with the Word. Believers can continually affirm the faith that is in their hearts by speaking God's Word, the answer, rather than speaking the problem. Talking about the problem can only make it worse, but talking about the answer will bring about its manifestation in your life.

V. SUMMARY—FAITH THAT SPEAKS

God wants His children to have and to use faith. "Without faith it is impossible to please Him" (Hebrews 11:6). But, God has given to each one of us a measure of faith and has told us the way in which we may develop and use that faith. God's Word is the source of any faith we now have, and it is the source of any increase of faith we may experience in the future.

To walk by faith means to exercise the faith that God has given us and to speak out of our mouths the Word of God. As we act on the Word, both by obeying its precepts and by confessing it daily, we will not only grow in faith, but we will receive from God's gracious hand all that He has given to us through the death of His Son.

God's will for His children is health, prosperity, victory, and complete deliverance from the power of the enemy. God wants us blessed in every area of our lives. But, we will only receive these blessings as we begin to put all our trust and confidence in God and His Word. Thus, one of the reasons that faith is pleasing to God the Father is that it makes us able to receive more and more of His blessings.

BELIEVE
CONFESS
RECEIVE

LESSON NINE

DAY ONE

FAITH'S CONFESSION—THE EXAMPLE OF GOD STUDY QUESTIONS

1. Show from the Bible that every Christian has faith.

   _____

   _____

2. How does faith come? (Give scriptures.)

   _____

   _____

   Give three examples, from the Bible, of this principle in operation. What happened in each instance?

   a. _____

   _____

   b. _____

   _____

   c. _____

   _____

3. In order for a believer to have faith in any particular area, what must that person know?

   _____

4. Briefly, how does faith grow? What two factors are essential to a faith that is strong and alive? In what ways has faith grown in your own life?

   _____

   _____

   _____

   _____

   _____

LESSON NINE

DAY TWO

FAITH'S CONFESSION—THE EXAMPLE OF GOD STUDY QUESTIONS

1. What is the discriminating factor between faith and "mental assent"?

   _____

2. In your own words, explain how corresponding actions demonstrated an inner assurance of the heart (i.e. faith) in each of these instances:

a. (Genesis 22:1-18)

   _____

b. (Luke 5:17-20)

   _____

c. (Luke 17:11-14)

   _____

d. (Matthew 14:25-32)

   _____

   Find one additional example from the Bible.

e. _____

   _____

3. How are those who merely hear the Word, but don't do it, deluded?

   _____

   At what point will their delusion be exposed?

   _____

LESSON NINE DAY THREE
FAITH'S CONFESSION—THE EXAMPLE OF GOD STUDY QUESTIONS

1. Read Luke 6:47-49. What is the major difference between the two men described in this passage?

    _____

    _____

    _____

2. Why are actions, in and of them selves, not faith? What must one do before he can become an effectual doer of the Word?

    _____

    _____

    _____

3. Briefly define the "God-kind of faith."

    _____

    _____

    _____

4. Why did God change Abram's name to Abraham? Explain how God was operating in the "spirit of faith" when He did so.

    _____

    _____

    _____

5. How would you respond to a person who said, "I won't say that I'm healed until I feel and see a difference? That would be lying!"? What scriptures would you show him?

    _____

    _____

    _____

LESSON NINE

DAY FOUR

FAITH'S CONFESSION—THE EXAMPLE OF GOD STUDY QUESTIONS

1. What does a person's speech reveal about him?

   _____

   _____

   _____

   _____

2. Even though one negative statement won't bring adversity or calamity, why is it still important for us not to make negative confessions? How can the principle set forth in Mark 11:23 work against a person?

   _____

   _____

   _____

   _____

3. What are the two purposes behind confessing God's Word? How do they relate to one another?

   a. _____

   b. _____

4. How do you see the difference between maintaining a positive confession and hiding or refusing to face problems?

   _____

   _____

   _____

   _____

Lesson TEN FAITH & PATIENCE: THE DESIGN OF GOD

Lesson TEN FAITH & PATIENCE: THE DESIGN OF GOD

I. INTRODUCTION 219

II. STEADFAST PATIENCE..219
    A. Confidence in God 220
        1. The fiery furnace
        2. David & God's faithfulness
    B. You Have Need of Patience 221
        1. Retaining your faith under trial
        2. Don't give up—HOLD ON!

III. STANDING AGAINST ADVERSITY 223
    A. The Source of Adversity...223
        1. The thief
        2. Satan's limited means of attack
    B. Count It All Joy 225
        1. Coping vs. deliverance
        2. Perfect and complete
    C. The Battle Ground of the Fight of Faith.................226
        1. Fear
        2. Despondency

IV. RECEIVING THROUGH FAITH AND PATIENCE....229
    A. Make A Decision...229
    B. Stand Against Your Adversary...............................230
    C. Give Attention to God's Word................................230
    D. Speak Only Words of Faith 231

V. SUMMARY—PATIENCE, CONFIDENCE, FAITH, THE
PROMISES & GOD'S FAITHFULNESS 231

Lesson TEN FAITH & PATIENCE: THE DESIGN OF GOD

I. INTRODUCTION

In Mark 11:24 Jesus established a principle of faith which gives us insight into how to receive the blessings that God desires us to have. "Therefore I say to you, all things for which you pray and ask, believe that you have received them, and they shall be yours." The principle is this we are to believe that we have received (past tense) before we have any physical evidence, and then they shall be ours (future tense).

There is often, however, a period of time between when we believe that we have received and when we see a manifestation in the physical realm. It is during this time that Christians are sorely tempted to waver and give up. That is when we need to stand steadfastly in faith, unwavering in our conviction that God has already answered our prayers. That is when we need to exercise patience, so that we may receive. The Bible says that we are to imitate those who through faith and patience inherit the promises of God (Hebrews 6:12). It is when patience is added to faith that a believer will be able to remain steadfast until he receives the manifestation of what he is believing for. Patience will enable him to keep his faith applied until he inherits God's promise.

There comes a time in every believer's life when he must stand firmly in faith and on the Word in the face of adversity and trial. Faith in God's Word is enough to carry a believer through any difficulty which the enemy can stir up. And faith will bring a person through a trial victoriously, if he remains patient and does not give up. When a believer perseveres in a trial, remaining steadfast and patient in faith, he will always come out the victor in every situation.

Faith is the spiritual quality which enables us to receive from God. But often, believers are tempted to give up their stand of faith when things don't appear to be going according to what they have believed. This is when patience (steadfastness or perseverance) is essential. Without patience no one would keep their faith engaged long enough to see the fulfillment of God's promise. "And we desire that each one of you show the same diligence so as to realize the full assurance of hope until the end, that you may not be sluggish, but imitators of those who through faith and patience inherit the promises" (Hebrews 6:11,12). If Abraham had not been patient as well as faithful, he would never have received the promise of God. But Abraham was a patient man. "And thus, having patiently waited, he obtained the promise" (Hebrews 6:15).

Patience is what keeps faith engaged until the fulfillment of the promise, or until the answer to the prayer is manifested in the physical realm. W. E. Vine's Expository Dictionary of New Testament Words defines patience as follows: "Patience is the quality that does not surrender to circumstances or succumb under trial; it is the opposite of despondency and is associated with hope." Patience enables a believer to stand until he experiences results.

When patience is added to faith, faith will stay engaged, and he will receive his inheritance from God. But, faith will not remain firm unless patience is put into effect in a believer's life.

A. CONFIDENCE IN GOD

"Do not, therefore, fling away your fearless confidence, for it carries a great and glorious compensation of reward" (Hebrews 10:35 Amplified). The fearless confidence to which the writer of Hebrews refers is our faith in God and His Word. It is our inner assurance that God's Word is true, and that He will not fail us. God's Word will not fail, if a believer will retain his confidence in it. These Hebrews were being tempted to fling away their confidence and trust in God.

If it is not cast away, fearless confidence (faith) has great reward attached to it. Standing in faith will bring to the believer all the things which God purchased for them through the redemptive work of His Son. Faith has a "great and glorious compensation of reward," because God is a rewarder of those who seek Him (Hebrews 11:6).

1. The fiery furnace

Read Daniel 3.

Shadrach, Meshach, and Abednego were three men who retained their confidence in God and His ability to deliver them. In the face of imminent fiery destruction, they boldly said to Nebuchadnezzar, "Our God whom we serve is able to deliver us from the furnace of blazing fire, and He will deliver us out of your hand O king" (Daniel 3:17). They didn't let the circumstances shake their confidence and faith in their God. They fully expected to come out of the furnace unscathed, before they even went in.

Their fearless confidence had a great compensation of reward. They were delivered from the evil intention of the king and unharmed by his attempt to destroy them, because they trusted in God to deliver them (Daniel 3:28). The end result of the trial was that the three Hebrews were promoted to positions of honor within Nebuchadnezzar's kingdom (Daniel 3:29, 30). They received the compensation that comes when a person puts his full trust and confidence in the Lord.

2. David & God's faithfulness

David's confidence was in God because he was convinced of God's mercy and faithfulness. "Thy loving kindness O Lord extends to the heavens, Thy faithfulness reaches to the skies" (Psalm 36:5). "Forever, O Lord, Thy word is settled in heaven. Thy faithfulness continues throughout all generations . . ."(Psalm 119:89, 90). David was assured of the fact that, no matter what the circumstances, his God was faithful to deliver him. That is why he constantly affirmed God's goodness in his own thinking. "Return to your rest, O my soul, for the Lord has dealt bountifully with you" (Psalm 116:7).

Our confidence in God is based upon a revelation of His goodness and faithfulness. In order to stand steadfast in faith, you must understand that God is unfailing and will not let you down if you're trusting in His faithfulness. The three Hebrews in Daniel knew that God would deliver them out of the hand of the wicked king; their confidence was in God and His faithfulness.

B. YOU HAVE NEED OF PATIENCE

"For you have need of steadfast patience and endurance, so that you may perform and fully accomplish the will of God and thus receive and carry away (and enjoy to the full) what is promised" (Hebrews 10:36 Amplified) Patience and endurance are the qualities which will keep a person from flinging away his confidence or faith in God and His goodness. Only patience will enable a person to keep his faith engaged, so that he can receive and carry away what God has promised in His Word.

A good example of the relationship between faith and patience is seen in the way in which a person brakes his car. Faith is like the brake that brings about the desired result (i.e. the stopping of the vehicle). Patience is like the foot that keeps the brake applied until the vehicle is brought to a complete halt. In the same way, faith brings about the desired result, but patience keeps faith applied, in the face of adverse circumstances, until the result is manifested. If a person flings away his confidence, it is like putting his foot to the brake of a car, but removing it before the car is brought to a stop.

1. Retaining your faith under trial

Patience does not surrender to circumstances or succumb under trial. It is in the midst of trial and adverse circumstances that a believer will be tempted to give up. No one is going to be tempted to fling away his confidence when everything is going right. But when circumstances arise which are contrary to God's Word and will, then the enemy comes to try to get believers to throw away their faith in God's faithfulness.

Without patience a believer will not, have the endurance to retain his faith when things are not going right. He will succumb under trial and surrender to circumstances (usually by saying that those circumstances are the will of God), and so will not receive the reward that God wants him to have. "But my righteous one shall live by faith, and if he shrinks back, my soul has no pleasure in him" (Hebrews 10:38). God has no pleasure in those who draw back (i.e. who throw away their confidence), because this stops the blessing of God from being manifested in their lives. God delights in the prosperity of His people (Psalm 35:27), and it is His good pleasure to give unto us the kingdom (Luke 12:32).

2. Don't give up—HOLD ON!

Every believer has need of patience, for without it, one would quickly give up under trial. Abraham stood firm in his conviction that God would honor His Word, and patiently waited in the face of insurmountable difficulty. It was his patience that caused him to remain steadfast on God's promise, even though what God had promised was not immediately manifested.

Even so, we must exercise our patience so that we can receive from God. Just because the promises of God are not immediately manifested in our experience is no reason for us to give up. When patience keeps faith applied, then the result will be forthcoming. But if we allow ourselves to become discouraged, then we will not leave our faith engaged long enough to see the manifestation of the things which God has promised. So the exhortation to the Hebrews is given also to **US**. Don't throw away your confidence in God and His Word! Faith and confidence have great reward, if they are retained steadfastly and not flung away because of discouragement.

III. STANDING AGAINST ADVERSITY

Patience is the power to hold oneself calm in the day of trial or adversity, and not be shaken off the Word. The day of adversity is that time in a believer's life when circumstances seem to contradict the Word of God. (It is sometimes called trial, testing, tribulation or the evil day.) In these times, the temptation comes for believers to cast away their faith in God's ability and faithfulness. But if one is trained out of the Word to be patient and not to give in, then he will not be shaken by the winds of adversity. "Blessed is the man whom You discipline and instruct, O Lord, and teach out of Your law; that you may give him power to hold himself calm in the days of adversity, until the [inevitable] pit of corruption is dug for the wicked" (Psalm 94:12,13 Amplified).

Patience has the courage to refuse what Satan's circumstances can prove true in the natural world. Patience says, "Let God be true but every man a liar!" (Romans 3:4 KJV) It won't fail under pressure, because it knows that God's Word has never failed. Patience knows that when faith is exercised on God's Word, success is inevitable. It is not moved by adverse circumstance or trial, but remains steadfast, trusting in God's Word and His goodness.

A. THE SOURCE OF ADVERSITY

When faced with tribulation and trial, it is imperative for Christians to understand that God is not the source of these things in their lives. God does not tempt (try or test) His people with adversity or calamity. "Let no man say when he is tempted, 'I am being tempted by God'; for God cannot be tempted by evil, and He Himself does not tempt anyone" (James 1:13).

Our real adversary, the one behind trial and adversity, is the devil and his demonic hosts. Satan is called our adversary (I Peter 5:8), because he is the one who is pitted against us. God is not against us; God is for us! (Romans 8:31, 32). "For our struggle is not against flesh and blood, but against the rulers, against the powers, against the world forces of this darkness, against the spiritual forces of wickedness in the heavenly places." (Ephesians 6:12). This verse shows us clearly that our adversaries are evil, demonic powers that seek to steal the Word from within us and make us cast away our confidence in God.

Paul goes on to say that we are to stand against the wiles of the enemy which he brings against us in the "evil day" (Ephesians 6:13), that time in our lives when the enemy comes against us with lying circumstances.

1. The thief

Jesus said that when the Word of God is planted within a person's heart, Satan comes immediately to steal what has been planted within them (Mark 4:15). The persecution and adversity arise in order to try to get the Word out of a believer (Mark 4:17). Satan will try to use trial and test to get us to fling away our confidence. Those trials will always come in the form of physical evidence which seems to contradict God's Word, and cast doubt on God's intentions toward us. Tribulation and adversity are nothing more than the enemy trying our faith. They are an attempt to get the Word (the basis of faith) out of our hearts. When a believer retains his confidence in God and His Word, there is no way that he can fail to receive from God. Because of this, the enemy tries everything within his limited power to get us to throw in the towel, by convincing us that the Word is not working, and that God will let us down.

2. Satan's limited means of attack

The only weapons which the enemy can level against us are natural weapons. Satan does not have the authority or ability to supernaturally overwhelm Christians. "No temptation has overtaken you but such as is common to man; but God is faithful, who will not allow you to be tempted beyond what you are able, but with the temptation will provide the way of escape also, that you may be able to endure it" (I Corinthians 10:13).

The enemy's tests are not overwhelmingly powerful; they are "common to man." This means that Satan's power against us is limited to natural means. He works his weapons against, us in the physical and mental realms. This is why he must use deception to accomplish his devices in the earth. If he were able to supernaturally overcome Christians at will, he would have done so long ago. But, Satan is not able to simply annihilate believers whenever he pleases. He must therefore deceive them into thinking that he can destroy them, and thus get them to throw away their faith and confidence. The enemy cannot rob a believer of his faith and confidence in God. The believer has to throw it away himself! Thus, Satan tries every day to deceive believers into thinking that he has the power to overwhelm them. Christians who believe this lie of the devil will always fling away their confidence.

B. COUNT IT ALL JOY

The scriptures exhort believers to count it as joy when they are tempted, tested or tried (Romans 5:3; James 1:2). We are not to rejoice because of adversity. We are to rejoice in the midst of trial because we know something about that trial.

The Bible says that adversity exercises and develops patience in the believer. "Because you know that the testing of your faith develops perseverance (patience)." (James 1:3 NIV) The joy comes from our knowing that any trial which we encounter can only make us stronger and more mature, if we will allow patience to work as it should.

"Perseverance must finish its work so that you may be mature and complete, not lacking anything" (James 1:4 NIV). The problem with many Christians is that they don't allow patience a chance to work, and so give up in the midst of the trial or adversity. But, the scriptures call upon us to be patient and to persevere in the midst of trial or tribulation (Romans 12:12). As we stand steadfast in the midst of trial, then patience is developed within us.

1. Coping vs. deliverance

The end result and aim of patience is that the promises of God be manifested in our lives. Some mistakenly believe that patience means the ability to bear with a situation which has no solution. Since there is no way out of the trial and adversity, patience is seen as the ability to cope with it. Thus, if one were sick, patience would enable a person to cope with the disease. But, Bible patience is given so that we can keep our faith engaged until the unchangeable situation changes by the power of God. Patience is meant to take us through adversity, not just to help us to cope. "The Lord knows how to rescue the godly from temptation" (II Peter 2:9). God's purpose and desire is that we experience deliverance from adversity in this life. Many relegate deliverance from temptations to the return of Jesus. But the Bible states that God will deliver us out of all our trials—in this life. Paul, in speaking of the many trials and adversities which he had faced during his ministry said, "Out of them [**ALL**] the Lord delivered me!" (II Timothy 3:11). "Many are the afflictions of the righteous; but the Lord delivers him out of them ALL!" (Psalm 34:19).

2. Perfect and complete

Jesus taught His disciples that they could rejoice while in the midst of tribulation. "In the world ye shall have tribulation; but be of good cheer; I have overcome the world" (John 16:33 KJV). It is a fact that as long as we are here on this earth, we will have trials and adversity. Jesus Himself said so. But He also told us to be of good cheer, because He had already overcome the world.

We can rejoice and count it all joy when we encounter tribulation, because we know that when patience is put to work, it will make us complete in Christ, and God will always make a way of escape for us.

He has overcome the world! Thus, we can face each trial with the full realization that not only will God deliver us from it, but also that the trial will develop patience within us. And when patience is allowed to have its full effect in our lives, then we will be perfect and complete, not lacking in anything (James 1:4).

C. THE BATTLE GROUND OF THE FIGHT OF FAITH

When faced with trial or tribulation, Christians often fail to recognize where the battle must be fought. The fight of faith is not an external, physical battle against adverse circumstances. The fight of faith is within the soul of each individual believer. The struggle is one of keeping our thinking and meditation stayed on God and His Word, rather than on the situation.

As we said earlier, the enemy's external attacks are attempts to get The Word out of us, so that we will give up and shrink back from our confidence. His real aim is to get the storm that is raging outside, within us, so that we will become fearful and despondent. This is exactly what happened to the disciples as they encountered a storm on the Sea of Galilee. They were overcome not by the storm so much as by their fear of the storm. They allowed the storm to get inside them. But Jesus was asleep in the rear of the ship; the storm did not get inside Him. He awoke and simply rebuked the wind and the waves (Mark 4:35-41).

What happened to the disciples in this situation often happens to believers today. They allow the storm of adversity to become lodged within them in the form of fear and despondency. They struggle against the outward manifestation of the enemy's attack, as the disciples surely must have tried to counter the effects of the storm by rowing and bailing. But, all the time they do not realize that they are losing the battle within. Jesus could speak to the wind and waves effectively because He had not allowed the storm to lodge within Him; He was not afraid! But the disciples were first fearful, and then they became despondent; they thought that they were going to die (Mark 4:38).

The two major inward attacks that Satan and his demons will wield against believers are fear and despondency. If he can win this inward battle by planting these two things within a believer, then he can get the believer to cast away his confidence. But if the believer will recognize the real source of the problem, and where the battleground really lies, fear and despondency will not be able to lodge themselves in his heart and mind. Circumstances will come into line if a believer will retain his confidence, not casting it away because of fear or despondency.

1. Fear

Fear is the opposite of faith; it operates in much the same manner as doe's faith, but brings about opposite results. Faith is our confidence in the truthfulness of God's Word. Fear is our belief in the lies of the devil. Faith is the assurance or substance of things hoped for or desired. Fear is the substance of things which are not desired.

The arena of faith is the mind, and the fight of faith is one of keeping the mind stayed on God and His Word. The enemy will attempt to destroy our confidence by planting thoughts of failure and disaster in our minds. He wants to get the storm within us through fear, as he did with the disciples. But, the Bible says that we are to keep our minds fixed on things that are true and of good report (Philippians 4:8). Certainly, the lies of the enemy do not qualify as "good" or of "good report." So when facing trial or adversity, the battle is fought within one's own mind. When the storm has been kept out of a person's mind, then he can squarely face physical obstacles and through the power of God overcome them.

2. Despondency

In W. E. Vine's definition of patience, despondency was listed as the opposite of patience. Just as fear is the opposite of' faith, so despondency is the opposite of patience. Despondency always grows out of a person's fear that the Word of God will fail them. It is the state of mind which will always give up and cast away confidence in God's Word. If the devil can convince a person—through fear—that they are bound to fail, and that God's Word will not work in a particular situation, then all that that person is left with is hopelessness and despair.

Despondency is the enemy of patience. It will do the exact opposite of what patience will do. Patience will enable a person to stand firm in faith, in the face of testing and trial. Despondency will cause a person to waver and vacillate on their faith, and eventually cause that person to cast away their faith.

As with fear, the battle with despondency is in one's mind. It is when people become convinced in their own minds that there is no hope that they give up.

Satan knows that he cannot simply overwhelm believers. If he is going to defeat them in any area, he must, through deception, get them to give up the fight and succumb to the trial. Thus, he comes against believers with fear and despondency, in order to get Christians to cast away their confidence in God. He can only win when he convinces someone of the lie that there is no hope and no answer. But, if a believer will not allow fear or despondency to remain within, but will patiently stand in faith, the enemy does not have the power to stop the manifestation of the answer or deliverance from the trial.

The fight of faith is an inward struggle, not an outward physical struggle. The enemy's aim is to get you to fling away your fearless confidence. When faced with trial or test remember that the real target is not your body or your possessions. **The real target is your faith and confidence in God and His Word.** That is the precious commodity which the devil wants to rob from you. Before attempting to address the physical 'situation, make sure that the storm has not become lodged within. If it has, deal with that inner storm of fear and discouragement first by reaffirming in your own thinking the goodness and faithfulness of God.

Meditate on the faithfulness of your Father until the storm is no longer within you, and that fear and despondency are cast out. Then address the situation by speaking a positive confession out of your mouth, just like Jesus did on the Sea of Galilee.

IV. RECEIVING THROUGH FAITH AND PATIENCE

The Bible says that Abraham received the promised son through faith and patience. Faith brought the impossible to pass, but patience kept faith engaged until the promised son was manifested in the physical realm. It is when we stand steadfastly on the Word of God that we receive from God what He has promised us. "Blessed is the man who perseveres under trial; for once he has been approved he will receive the crown of life, which the Lord has promised to those who love Him" (James 1:12). The one who perseveres under trial, and doesn't cast away his confidence is the one who receives.

The following are four steps to follow in standing steadfastly in faith for the things that we desire. These are not given as some kind of formula. They are simply given to help us understand how to remain steadfast and unmovable in our faith, so that the devil cannot deceive or defeat us.

A. MAKE A DECISION

Make a decision to believe you receive when you pray and decide not to change (Mark 11:24). Don't look to the physical realm for your evidence of answered prayer. The answer is yours in the spiritual realm as soon as you believe that you have received. Your evidence of the answer is God's

Wore alone. Make a decision not to change your confession, until you see your answer come to pass in the physical realm.

Patience will enable you to stand on God's Word, unwavering, and will keep your faith engaged, until the manifestation comes. Make a decision to win! A decision is an exercise of your will. The dictionary defines "will" as "strong purpose, intention or determination." If you make a determination to have what God's Word says, you will have it. Will is the determination to receive something. Make a decision to stand with the determination that you are going to come through every trial victoriously!

B. STAND AGAINST YOUR ADVERSARY

"Submit yourselves therefore to God. Resist the devil, and he will flee from you" (James 4:7). Too often, Christians will resist the Word of God with their mouth (through negative confessions), and submit themselves to the devil, by confessing and meditating on his lies. But, we must submit ourselves to God by meditating on what He has said, and resist the lies and evil thoughts of Satan.

Learn to stop worrying. Worry is meditation on Satan's words. Meditate on God's Word instead. When a though' comes to you, discern its origin. Not every thought originates in you. If a thought is contrary to the truth of God's Word, it is a lie from the enemy. Resist the devil by rejecting his lies one at a time in the Name of Jesus.

The Bible tells us to control what we think about (Philippians 4:8). In this way, we resist the onslaughts of the adversary.

C. GIVE ATTENTION TO GOD'S WORD

"My son, give attention to my words; incline your ear to my sayings. Do not let them depart from your sight; keep them in the midst of your heart. For they are life to those that find them and health to all their whole body" (Proverbs 4:2022). Keep the Word in your heart. Pay attention to it. If your attention is on what God says and not on what the devil is saying, he doesn't have any way of defeating you. We are instructed to do these three things:

• Keep the Word in our ears.

• Keep the Word in front of our eyes.

• Keep the Word in the midst of our hearts.

1f you are going to win, you will have to give attention to God's Word! Just as no human being can look in two different directions at the same time, so also we cannot look attentively at God's Word and the devil's lies simultaneously. You are either looking at or giving attention to the Word of God, or you are giving attention to circumstances and the lies of the enemy. If you give attention to what the devil says, fear will arise in your heart. But if you give your attention to the Word of God, faith will arise in your heart. If you will keep your attention focused on God's Word—all the time—then you put yourself into a position where you see every circumstance and nation through the eye of faith. The eye of faith sees the thing as already accomplished, provided through the death and resurrection of Jesus.

D. SPEAK ONLY WORDS OF FAITH

Refuse to speak words contrary to what you believe that you have received. Speak only words of success and abundance. Very often believers are defeated because of the words which come out of their mouths they speak only what they can see in the physical and this affirms what the enemy is trying to prove to them that the Word isn't going to work this time. Our words must always be those which affirm that we have the answer. These words will arise out of a heart that is assured of God's faithfulness to His Word. Just as faith always finds expression out of a person's mouth, so fear and doubt always find expression out of the mouth. Thus, we must take heed to what comes forth from our mouths, and be certain that what we speak is in line with the Word of God and with the answer that we desire.

V. SUMMARY—PATIENCE, CONFIDENCE, FAITH, THE PROMISES & GOD'S FAITHFULNESS

There is never any reason for a believer to cast away his confidence in God and His Word. God is faithful and true to the promises which He has given us in the scriptures. "Thy loving kindness, O Lord, extends to the heavens, Thy faithfulness reaches to the skies" (Psalm 36:5). God's mercy and His faithfulness are infinite. Because of this fact, His Word can be fully trusted and is worthy of complete confidence. But believers must learn to exercise patience, so that their faith in God will stay applied, and so that they don't cast away their confidence (Hebrews 10:36). Without patience, confidence will eventually be cast away, and the promises of God will not be received.

LESSON TEN

DAY ONE

FAITH & PATIENCE—THE DESIGN OF GOD
STUDYQUESTIONS

1. What is the principle of faith put forth in Mark 11:24?

   _____

   _____

2. Why is patience essential? What would happen to a Christian if he didn't

   _____

   _____

3. Why did David have such trust and confidence in God? (Give scripture.) How does this revelation affect your faith in God and His Word?

   _____

   _____

4. What does each of the following scriptures show us about faith and/or patience?

a. Hebrews 6:11, 12

   _____

   _____

b. Hebrews 10:35

   _____

   _____

d. James 1:4

   _____

   _____

e. James 1:12

   _____

   _____

LESSON TEN

DAY TWO

FAITH & PATIENCE—THE DESIGN OF GOD

STUDYQUESTIONS

1. Why does God have no pleasure in those who "draw back"?

   _____

   _____

2. What is the exhortation given to us in Hebrews 10:35?

   _____

   _____

   Why is it advantageous for us to heed that exhortation?

   _____

   _____

3. Who is the source of temptation and trial? What is his real aim in sending these trials? (Give scriptures.)

   _____

   _____

4. Explain the enemy's tactics against believers. Can he supernaturally overwhelm any believer at will? What are his weapons against us?

   _____

   _____

   _____

5. What is the difference between exercising Bible patience in a situation and merely coping with that situation?

   _____

   _____

   _____

LESSON TEN

DAY THREE

FAITH & PATIENCE—THE DESIGN OF GOD
STUDYQUESTIONS

1. How many temptations and afflictions does the Lord deliver us from in this life? (Give 2 scriptures to support your answer.)

   _____

   _____

   _____

2. What is the fight of faith, and where is it fought?

   _____

   _____

   _____

3. Read Mark 4:35-41.

a. Explain what mistake the disciples made in dealing with that trial How is it similar to what many Christians do today?

   _____

   _____

   _____

b. How did Jesus' response differ from that of the disciples? What does His response say to you if you were to face a trial?

   _____

   _____

   _____

4. What are the two major inward attacks that Satan brings against us?

a. _____

b. _____

LESSON TEN

DAY FOUR

FAITH & PATIENCE—THE DESIGN OF GOD
STUDYQUESTIONS

1. List four basic steps necessary in standing steadfastly in faith for the things which we desire.

    a. _____

    b. _____

    c. _____

    d. _____

2. Define "worry."

    _____

    _____

    What can we do to counter it?

    _____

    _____

3. In the future, how will you resist the enemy? What steps will you take toward off his inward and outward attacks? On what will you base your confidence? Give three scriptures on which you will stand.

    _____

    _____

    _____

    _____

4. Briefly explain James 1:24, in light of what you have learned from this lesson.

    _____

    _____

    _____

    _____

Lesson ELEVEN HEALING: THE WILL OF GOD

Lesson ELEVEN HEALING: THE WILL OF GOD

I. INTRODUCTION 241

II. GOD'S WILL IS HEALING 242
   A. God's Redemptive Names...242
     1. The unchanging nature of Jehovah-Rapha
     2. The testimony of Jehovah-Rapha
   B. The Ministry of Jesus 245
     1. Motivated by His compassion
     2. Motivated by His mission
     3. Motivated by His enemy
   C. The New Testament Church 248
   D. The Will of God Today...248

III. HEALING IN THE ATONEMENT...249
   A. Healing in Old Testament Types 249
     1. The Jubilee
     2. The bronze serpent
   B. Christ's Atonement: Prophesied and Fulfilled 251
     1. Grief's and sorrows/sickness and pain
     2. Our diseases carried away
     3. Redemption from sin and sickness
   C. Is Healing for All? 253

IV. SOME COMMON OBJECTIONS 253
   A. What About Job?...254
     1. The accusing afflicter—Satan
     2. The source of sickness—Satan
     3. Our redemption from sickness—Jesus
   B. Paul's Thorn 256
     1. Persecution
     2. Suffering for Jesus?

V. SUMMARY—THE CURSE AND THE BLESSING—GETTING THE FACTS STRAIGHT 258

Lesson ELEVEN HEALING: THE WILL OF GOD

I. INTRODUCTION

For many centuries, the concept of divine healing has been lost from the Christian Church. Theologians and philosophers have relegated it to another age or dispensation, asserting that God only healed in the Church's early history. According to these scholars, one cannot expect this blessing to be manifested today, because God simply does not move in such a way any longer. Yet, the Word of God has never changed. For all these centuries, it has proclaimed the same Gospel which Jesus and the apostles proclaimed in Jerusalem, Judea, Samaria and the uttermost parts of the earth. The Gospel which God has spoken through the Word is one of complete salvation. "For I am not ashamed of the gospel, for it is the power of God for salvation, to everyone who believes" (Romans 1:16) Dr. C. I. Scofield, editor of The Scofield Reference Bible, declares: "The Hebrew and Greek words for salvation imply the ideas of deliverance, safety, preservation, healing and soundness. Salvation is the great inclusive word of the Gospel, gathering into itself all the redemptive acts and processes."

When Jesus came proclaiming the Gospel (good news), it was a gospel of deliverance from bondage of every kind. Thus we see that everywhere Jesus went, He healed the sick and set the captive free. When He commissioned His disciples, He charged them to do exactly the same, to preach and to heal the sick (Matthew 10:7, 8).

After Jesus' ascension, the apostles continued the same ministry of preaching and healing (Acts 5:12, 15). In fact, wherever the New Testament records the proclaiming of the Gospel, either by Jesus Himself or by His disciples and apostles, it also records the healing of the sick (Luke 6:17-19; Luke 10:9; Acts 8:6,7).

Today, healing is just as much a part of the Gospel of Jesus Christ as it was in the days of the early church. Jesus proclaimed release to the captives, as did His disciples after Him. Although this part of the Gospel has faded from the thinking of many Christians, it has never faded from the pages of God's Word. The Word clearly records that the preaching of the Gospel was always accompanied by the healing power of God.

Preaching the Gospel and healing the sick always went hand-in-hand. Any gospel which leaves out healing is less than the gospel which Jesus preached. Preaching the full-gospel of Jesus must include proclaiming healing to those who are in need of that deliverance.

II. GOD'S WILL IS HEALING

God is a healing God, One whose perfect will is for His people to live in health. He has always made provision for healing and health among His people. This is true under both the New and Old Covenants. Under the Old Covenant, God promised to remove all sickness from the children of Israel, if they would remain faithful to Him (Deuteronomy 7:15). God placed before them a choice: life or death, blessing or cursing. The choice was theirs, but God made His will perfectly clear. He said, "Choose life!" (Deuteronomy 30:19). No matter what they chose, God's desire remained the same; He wanted the children of Israel to have healing and life instead of sickness and death. God's will is healing. It is as much His will to heal sick bodies, as it is to save the lost. Healing of men's bodies is as much a part of God's redemptive action as the saving of men's souls. It is never God's perfect will for His people to experience sickness. Sometimes, men's sin and disobedience will bring judgment in the form of sickness. But, this doesn't change the fact that God's perfect will is still healing and deliverance. God's promise is that if a person will repent and turn, He will extend His healing power, as He had always wanted to, and bring deliverance.

The will of God with regard to healing and health is explicit in both the Old and New Testaments. God never changes. Healing was, is and will be His perfect will so long as men are in need of it. In the Old Testament, healing is found to be a part of God's redemptive name, Jehovah-Rapha. In the New Testament, Jesus came showing exactly who God is and what He is like (Hebrews 1:3). Jesus healed the sick wherever He went, thus proclaiming to all that God's will is healing.

A. GOD'S REDEMPTIVE NAMES

In the Old Testament the Hebrew word for "God" (Jehovah) expresses His redemptive character. "Jehovah" means "the self-existent one," and is used in those scriptures which refer to God's redemption of man.

"Jehovah is distinctly the redemption name of Deity" Seven times in the Old Testament, the name "Jehovah" is joined with another Hebrew word, yielding a compound name which gives us a deeper insight into God's nature. These compound names of Jehovah each reveal a distinct aspect of God's redemptive nature. "In His redemptive relation to man, Jehovah has seven compound names which reveal Him as meeting every need of man from his lost state to the end."

The seven redemptive compound names of God are:

- **Jehovah-Jireh**—"the Lord will provide" (Genesis 22:13, 14) Reveals God's redemptive role as provider, especially with reference to His ultimate provision for man, Jesus Christ.

- **Jehovah-Rapha**—"the Lord that heals" (Exodus 15:26). The context of this verse shows clearly that this means physical healing.

- **Jehovah-Nissi**—"the Lord our banner" or "victory" (Exodus 17:15). Christ is our victory over the enemy, and the cross our banner.

- **Jehovah-Shalom**—"the Lord our peace" (Judges 6:24). God redeemed us from enmity with Him through Jesus Christ, so that we now have "peace with God" (Romans 5:1).

- **Jehovah-Raah**—"the Lord my shepherd" (Psalm 23:1). Jesus is the "Good Shepherd" who laid down His life for the sheep.

- **Jehovah-Tsidkenu**—"the Lord our righteousness" (Jeremiah 23:6). Through Jesus, we have become the righteousness of God in Him.

- **Jehovah-Shammah**—"the Lord is present" (Ezekiel 48:35). God's abiding presence is always with His people, for He has promised never to leave or forsake them.

As we have said, each of these redemptive names shows us a distinct aspect of God in His relation to and dealings with men. While they are all equally important, here we will discuss specifically the name "Jehovah-Rapha," since healing is the subject at hand.

1. The unchanging nature of Jehovah-Rapha

When God named Himself "Jehovah-Rapha," He revealed an unchanging element of His character. **Healing is in the very nature of God**. There is perhaps no greater statement as to God's will in this matter, than that of His name. God is "the Lord that heals." As Jehovah-Rapha, His will is to see the sick healed and the maimed restored.

Thus it was that God promised the children of Israel, "But you shall serve the Lord your God, and He will bless your bread and your water; and I will remove sickness from your midst. There shall be no one miscarrying or barren in your land; I will fulfill the number of your days" (Exodus 23:25, 26). The children of Israel were promised the blessing of perfect health, if they would walk according to God's statutes. "You shall be blessed above all peoples; there shall be no male or female barren among you or among your cattle. And the Lord will remove from you all sickness; and He will not put on you any of the harmful diseases of Egypt which you have known, but He will lay them on all who hate you" (Deuteronomy 7:14, 15) This didn't pertain to some of the Israelites, but to all of them. As a nation and a people, the Israelites were provided with healing and health from Jehovah-Rapha.

The Bible records that when Israel came out of Egypt, after years of oppression and physical abuse, there was not one feeble person among their tribes (Psalm 105:37). And even though future generations of Israelites didn't experience this blessing because of sin and disobedience, yet God remained Jehovah-Rapha, and His will for them was undeviating. God's desire was that His people would live their lives in health and strength and so "fulfill the number of their days."

2. The testimony of Jehovah-Rapha

Careful reading of the Old Testament will show that God moved in His capacity as Jehovah-Rapha many times during Israel's history. King Hezekiah was sick to the point of death; he prayed to the Lord, and God healed him (II Kings 20:1-5). The Shunammite woman received her son back from the dead because she interceded with Elisha, the man of God (II Kings 4). Even Naaman the Syrian (a Gentile) was able to avail himself of God's healing power to cure his leprosy (II Kings 5:1-3, 14).

No matter what judgment the sin of Israel incurred for them, God's will to heal was always present. When repentance was made, healing came.

Thus David could say, "Bless the Lord, O my soul, and forget none of His benefits; Who pardons all your iniquities; Who heals all your diseases" (Psalm 103:2,3). "Then they cried unto the Lord in their trouble; He saved them out of their distresses. He sent His Word and healed them, and delivered them from their destructions" (Psalm 107:19, 20).

Under the Old Covenant, God's will was healing. Throughout the Old Testament, God proved Himself to be Jehovah-Rapha! His actions matched His redemptive name and were a testimony to His perfect will for men.

B. THE MINISTRY OF JESUS

Jesus is in every way a reflection of the Father God. Everything Jesus did while conducting His earthly ministry did at the impulse and example of the Father. The Bible says that Jesus exactly represents God (Hebrews 1:3), because He is God. Thus, whatever Jesus did during His earthly ministry was an express manifestation of God's will; **Jesus was the will of God in action on the earth!**

Jesus' earthly ministry is a profound statement about the will of God in healing. The apostle Peter summed up Jesus' entire ministry by saying, "You know of Jesus of Nazareth, how God anointed Him with the Holy Spirit and with power, and how **He went about doing good, and healing all who were oppressed by the devil;** for God was with Him" (Acts Acts 10:38). Wherever Jesus went, He healed the sick. This was a major part of His ministry. Through Jesus, God was letting it be known that He wanted people free from the oppression of disease. Jesus treated disease as an enemy, because that is how God views it. All the miracles, and healing, wonders which Jesus performed by the power of the Holy Spirit, He did at the impulse of the heavenly Father.

1. Motivated by His compassion
Jesus' motivation for healing the sick was more than just confirmation of His ministry. His ministry was indeed substantiated by the mighty works done at His hands, but a few spectacular miracles in key towns would have sufficed for that purpose. But Jesus healed the sick wherever He went. And repeatedly, the Gospel writers record that Jesus healed all that came to Him in need of deliverance (Matthew 12:15; 9:35; 14:35, 36; Luke 6:19). If

verification of His ministry were the only motivation behind the healings which Jesus accomplished, then He would not have needed to heal all in the vast multitudes that came to Him. But Jesus healed the sick because He had compassion on them, a compassion which flowed from the heart of God toward the sick and suffering.

"And when He went ashore, He saw a great multitude, and felt compassion for them, and healed their sick" (Matthew 14:14) It was His compassion for the sick that moved Jesus to heal (Matthew 20:33, 34).

It was His compassion for the oppressed multitude which prompted Him to send out His disciples equipped to preach and heal every kind of disease (Matthew 9:35-10:1). God's compassion and mercy are the underlying reasons for His willingness to heal. This Jesus demonstrated time and again during His earthly ministry.

2. Motivated by His mission

Jesus described His mission on the earth in one of the first sermons that He ever preached. He quoted the prophet Isaiah, saying of Himself, "The Spirit of the Lord is upon me, because He has anointed me to preach the gospel to the poor. He has sent me to proclaim release to the captives, and recovery of sight to the blind, to set free those who are downtrodden, to proclaim the favorable year of the Lord" (Luke 4:18, 19).

Both spiritually and temporally, Jesus came to free men from oppression and bondage. That is why God sent Him. Throughout the Gospels, we see that Jesus fulfilled that call. Everywhere He went, Jesus was willing to heal all those that came to Him. He simply carried out the will of the One who had sent Him. "For I have come down from heaven, not to do my own will, but the will of Him that sent me" (John 6:38) Jesus affirmed that He only did those things which He saw the Father doing (John 5:19).

Jesus was a living example of the will of God. "He who has seen me has seen the Father" (John 14:9). Watching Jesus in action is watching God in action. Jesus' willingness to heal all who came to Him is an unmistakable expression of God's will for the sick. God wants the sick to be healed! He commissioned Jesus to release those who were bound and oppressed. This ministry Jesus began while on the earth and consummated on the cross. As we shall see, Jesus' atoning death made the way for all men to be free from the oppression of the devil, brought on by sin. Through His Son (who was God manifest in the flesh), the Father declared to the world His divine will. Jesus went about "doing Good, and healing all who were oppressed of the devil," because **it is God's will that all men be free from the Satanic oppression of sickness.**

3.   Motivated by His enemy

Jesus' ministry sheds light on another fact that greatly needs clarification: Sickness is a curse from the devil—an enemy of God and man. This fact is not seen clearly in the Old Testament, because the concept of the enemy (the devil, Satan) was not yet fully revealed to the people of God. References to Satan in the Old Testament are few. But in the New Testament, the fight against wicked spiritual forces is vividly portrayed This is nowhere more evident than in Jesus' dealings with demons and with sickness Jesus viewed sickness as oppression, from which He, in His compassion, desired to set men free All during His earthly ministry, Jesus came against and destroyed the works which Satan had brought about in people's lives.

Once, in a synagogue, Jesus encountered a woman who was bent double with a condition caused by an evil spirit After He had healed her, He said to those standing by, "And this woman, a daughter of Abraham as she is, **whom Satan has bound** for eighteen long years, **should she not have been released from this bond** on the Sabbath day?" (Luke 13:16) Jesus labeled sickness as **bondage,** caused by Satan He emphatically asserted that this covenant woman of Israel had the right to be free from the enemy's bond This was Jesus attitude to all who came to Him in need of healing; they were satanically oppressed and needed to be released by the power of God. Thus, Peter summed up Jesus' ministry by saying that He did good and healed all that were oppressed by the devil (Acts 10:38).

Jesus said, "The thief comes only to steal, and kill, and destroy; I came that they might have life, and might have it abundantly" (John 10:10). He draws a clear line of demarcation. God's will is healing and blessing, and everything else that goes along with "abundant life." But if anything kills, steals, or destroys, then it has been labeled by Jesus as being from the enemy.

C. THE NEW TESTAMENT CHURCH

The ministry of the New Testament Church differs little from that of Jesus Himself. The record of the Church's beginning, the Acts of the Apostles, shows that Jesus' followers continued the same ministry of preaching and healing that the Lord had begun. The healing power of God and God's willingness to heal didn't ascend into heaven with Jesus. Jesus said before He left, "These signs will accompany those who have believed: . . . they will lay hands on the sick, and they will recover" (Mark 16:17, 18). Careful study of the book of Acts will reveal that this is exactly what happened. Everywhere the Gospel was preached, miracles of healing were performed (Acts 5:12, 15, 16; 8:7; 9:33, 34; 14:8-10; 19:11, 12; 28:8.9).

D. THE WILL OF GOD TODAY

God revealed His will for healing under the Old Covenant, telling the children of Israel, "The Lord will remove from you all sickness." He also gave them His covenant redemptive name, **Jehovah-Rapha: the Lord that heals.** Jesus came to do the will of Jehovah-Rapha on the earth; He demonstrated to all that God is a healing God. The Bible says that God is the same yesterday, today, and forever (Hebrews 13:8). He is still Jehovah-Rapha today under the New Covenant. It is as much His will for us, His covenant people, to walk in divine health as it was for the children of Israel to do so. The promise of health and healing still stands today. **God has not withdrawn it!**

It always has been, and always will be, God's will to heal the sick, as much as it is His will to save the lost. This fact must become firmly implanted in a person's thinking, if he wants to receive healing from the Lord. God hasn't withdrawn the physical benefits which He made available to the children of Israel. The New Covenant is a better covenant than the Old, more sure and steadfast. It is, therefore, absurd to think that God would withdraw this divine blessing when instituting a New Covenant with man. He hasn't changed since the days of Moses when He promised to "remove all sickness" from us, so that we could walk in perfect health.

III. HEALING IN THE ATONEMENT

The most profound statement as to God's will for healing is found in the atoning work of Jesus Christ. The Bible teaches that Jesus' substitutionary work on the cross includes the removal of sickness as well as the removal of sin. All will agree that whatever God has purchased on the cross, He wants all His children to possess. There is no Christian who would claim that God wants only some to be saved; Jesus died for the sins of the whole world (I John 2:2). What was done on Calvary was done for all men, not just for some. The blessings of God which are offered as a result of the cross are universal. It is important to realize that the blessing of healing promised to the children of Israel under the Old Covenant was bestowed on the basis of Calvary. God was able to forgive sins under that Covenant because of what Jesus would do on the cross (Romans 3:25; Hebrews 9:15). In the same way, God healed under that Old Covenant because Jesus was going to bear sickness and disease. In fact, no redemptive blessing can be obtained apart from the redemptive work of God's Son. All of God's redemptive names bespeak a privilege which only the cross could purchase. Thus, God's activities as Jehovah-Rapha (the Lord that heals) are accomplished on the basis of Calvary's atoning work.

By linking bodily healing with the atonement, the Bible shows beyond doubt that sickness is not the will of God; He wants all to be well. Sickness is an oppressive result of man's fall, from which God in His mercy sent His Son to deliver us.

A. HEALING IN OLD TESTAMENT TYPES

Throughout the Old Testament, healing is linked to atonement. When the children of Israel were plagued because of their sin, Aaron made atonement, and the plague was checked (Numbers 16:46-48). The punishment for their sin was stayed by the work of atonement which Aaron wrought when he stood between the dead and the living. In the book of Leviticus, the law stated that the cleansing of a leper was not complete until atonement had been made by the High Priest (Leviticus 14:18-20).

All the sacrifices of the Old Covenant which effected atonement are types and symbols of Jesus' sacrifice on the cross. The people's sins were forgiven by these sacrifices because the animal sacrifices foreshadowed Christ's ultimate atoning work. In the same way, when atonement was made, the people were healed, because those atoning sacrifices which brought about healing also foreshadowed Christ's death at Calvary.

1. The Jubilee

The Jubilee was a time of restoration which God established in the Jewish calendar. It was a year-long period, occurring every fifty years, in which every man was returned to his original possessions, and all captives were set free (Leviticus 25). This was the time of liberty and restoration which Jesus proclaimed in Luke 4:18-19, quoting the prophet Isaiah, "He has sent me to proclaim release to the captives, and recovery of sight to the blind, to set free those who are downtrodden, to proclaim the favorable year of the Lord." The "favorable year of the Lord" is this year of Jubilee.

Jesus came declaring that the Jubilee was a time of healing and restoration, both physically and spiritually. But in the year of Jubilee, no blessing or restoration, no liberty or release was proclaimed until the blast of the trumpet on the Day of Atonement. Jubilee began on the Day of Atonement (Leviticus 25:9). No captives went free, and no one received his land back until the sacrifices of atonement had been made. Even so today, no Gospel blessing is offered or bestowed irrespective of Jesus' atoning death. Jesus' Jubilee of release from sin, sickness and bondage of all forms is the direct result of His final atonement.

2. The bronze serpent

Read Numbers 21:5-9.

When the children of Israel murmured against Moses and against God, they were plagued with fiery serpents whose bites were fatal. But they were healed if they only looked upon the bronze serpent which Moses had fashioned at the Lord's command. Here we see that God's people were healed by looking upon a type of Jesus' death on the cross. (In John 3:14, Jesus made direct reference to this incident, saying that He was the fulfillment of that Old Testament type.) As the people looked steadfastly at the type of Jesus, they were made whole. The same is figuratively true today. Those who look steadfastly at what Jesus accomplished on the cross and meditate on that sacrifice will be made whole, just as the children of Israel were made whole. The bronze serpent on the staff was a symbol of atonement (i.e. Jesus' atonement), and that symbol of atonement brought about healing and deliverance for the afflicted Israelites.

B. CHRIST'S ATONEMENT: PROPHESIED AND FULFILLED

Read Isaiah 53.

Jesus' suffering and death at the hands of godless men were prophesied any hundreds of years before Jesus was even born. In the 22nd Psalm, David clearly depicts the suffering of Jesus on the cross. Numerous other Old Testament scriptures prophetically tell of the things which befell Jesus during His suffering and death (Psalm 41:9; Zechariah 11:12; Zechariah 12:10; Isaiah 50:6). But of all the prophecies describing The Lord's passion, one stands out in its detail and scope. The "53rd chapter of Isaiah is a graphic description of all that Jesus. Suffered and accomplished in His atoning work on the cross. This is known as the "Great Atonement Chapter" of the Old Testament, because it points directly to Calvary and what was accomplished there. It is not surprising to find that in this great chapter about atonement, redemption from sickness is found side by side with forgiveness for and release from sin. Christ's death is seen as being effectual to release from both sin and sickness.

1. Grief's and sorrows/sickness and pain

Careful study of the 3rd, 4th, and 10th verses of this chapter will show that these particular passages refer directly to Jesus bearing and carrying away the disease and sickness which came as a result of sin. (A study Bible with a marginal reading will verify this fact.) The words which are translated "grief's" and "sorrows" are respectively the Hebrew words "choli" and "makob." "Choli" means "sickness" and is so translated predominantly throughout the New American Standard Version of the Old Testament Only in Isaiah 53 is it rendered "grief." "Makob" means "pain," and is translated this way in most instances in the New American Standard Version of the Old Testament. Only three times is it rendered "sorrows," two of those times in Isaiah 53.

Thus, we could rightfully translate Isaiah **53**:3, **4,** and **10** in the following way:

3. **He was despised, and forsaken of men, A man of pains, and acquainted with sickness; and like one from whom men hide their face, He was despised, and we did not esteem Him.**
4. **Surely our sickness He Himself bore,**

10. But the Lord was pleased
To crush Him, He made Him sick.

(These are the marginal readings of both the King James and New American Standard Versions.)

That sickness and pain is part of what Jesus bore on the cross is indisputable, on the basis of this passage of scripture. Christ's atoning work on the cross covers all our sicknesses and diseases, as well as our sin.

2. Our diseases carried away

The New Testament itself verifies this translation of Isaiah 53:4, applying it directly to Jesus' ministry of healing those that were sick. We are told in the Gospel of Matthew that Jesus healed all who were ill "in order that what was spoken through Isaiah the prophet might be fulfilled, saying 'He Himself took our infirmities, and carried away our diseases" (Matthew 8:17).

Jesus' earthly healing ministry was a forerunner of His bearing sickness on the cross, just as His forgiving of sins was a forerunner of His bearing sin on the cross (Matthew 9:2,6). The words of Isaiah were fulfilled on Calvary, when Jesus bore not only our sins, but also all of our diseases. Jesus bore the full brunt of our sin—and the results of our sin. "Christ redeemed us from the curse of the Law, having become a curse for us" (Galatians 3:13). The curse of the Law, as listed in Deuteronomy, Chapter 28, includes every form of disease that exists, Christ redeemed us from sickness by having all our sickness and pains laid on Him; He bore the curse of sickness so that we wouldn't have to.

3. Redemption from sin and sickness

Thus the New Testament, as well as the Old Testament, bears witness to the fact that Calvary's redemption includes release from the oppression of sickness. The Jubilee which Jesus proclaimed was a Jubilee of release from sin, sickness, poverty, and from every other form of bondage which the devil had held man under for so many centuries Release from sin and release from sickness cannot be separated; they are both part and parcel of the work of atonement. Thus Peter says, "And He Himself bore our sins in His body on the cross that we might die to sin and live to righteousness, for by His wounds you were healed" (I Peter 2:24).

Here, redemption from sin and sickness are found side by side the same connection is made by the apostle James in his epistle. "And the prayer offered in faith will make the sick person well, the Lord will raise him up If he has sinned, he will be forgiven" (James 5:15 New International Version).

Both Peter and James saw forgiveness of sins and healing of to the body as being accomplished by the same work of Jesus, His death on the cross When Jesus redeemed us from sin, He also redeemed us from the curse of sickness and disease!

C. IS HEALING FOR ALL?

The answer to this question is an emphatic Yes' We have shown that God's will is to heal, He sent His only Son to die so that we could be freed from sin and sickness Nothing speaks more strongly to the universality of God's will for healing (that is, that He offers it to all who are afflicted) than the atonement As we have said, whatever was purchased on Calvary, was purchased for all There is no discrimination at the foot of the cross "Whoever will call upon the name of the Lord will be saved" (Romans 10:13), whether in spirit, mind or body.

Thus, to say that God will heal some, but not others, is tantamount to saying that God will save some, but not others It is God's will that all be saved, and come to the knowledge of the truth (II Peter 3:9); this is so because spiritual salvation was purchased through the atonement **Physical healing is as much a part of the atonement as forgiveness of sin, and so is also offered to all who are, in need.**

IV. SOME COMMON OBJECTIONS

We would do well to discuss some common misconceptions about healing which are prevalent among Christians today. It is widely accepted, today, that although God is able to heal, He many times withholds healing so that He may be glorified thereby. It is thought that sickness brings glory to God by the patient suffering of the one afflicted. Sickness is thus often viewed by these as a blessing from God, because good is sometimes the result of a person's illness. It is often said, "My illness made me turn to God!" or "While I was in the hospital, people were saved as a result of my witnessing!" Doubtless, good can come from illness, because God causes all things to work together for good to those who love God, to those who are called according to His purpose (Romans 8:28). God is merciful, and can turn any situation around to blessing and good, if we allow Him. But, this does not mean that God is the one behind the sickness, or that disease is divinely appointed.

Two major scriptural passages are used in connection with this idea of divinely appointed illness: the story of Job and Paul's thorn in the flesh. These two accounts are often raised as objections to the teaching that God's will is healing for all. Ignorance and misunderstanding of these two scriptures have kept many under the bondage of disease, thinking that they were glorifying God because of their affliction. Closer examination of these scriptures, along with comparison of other scriptures on healing, will show that they do not teach sickness as a "blessing" from God. The Bible is clear in its labeling of sickness as a curse, and not a blessing.

A. WHAT ABOUT JOB?

One common objection to healing that arises is the idea that God afflicted righteous Job. Many Christians feel that they cannot be healed, because they are just like Job: suffering at the command of God for some unknown divine purpose. This is an unfortunate misinterpretation of the book of Job. Job's story is by no means simple; it has been wrestled with for centuries by Jews and Christians alike. No simplistic answer is sufficient to explain all that happened to him. Whatever one may conclude from Job's experience, it is not sufficient Evidence from which to say that the will of God is sickness for anyone to say that God wants people sick on the basis of Job's experience is an oversimplification, and denies what God has said elsewhere in the Word concerning healing.

1. The accusing afflicter—Satan

Job, according to the scriptures, was "blameless, upright, fearing God, and turning from evil" (Job 1:1). Yet, there befell him numerous grievous calamities. During all these calamities, Job did not curse God, as Satan said he would (Job 1:22; 2:10). Job's comforters judged that Job's calamity was the result of some hidden sin. Job steadfastly rejected this idea, always asserting his own uprightness before God. Yet both Job and his comforters were ignorant of what had transpired in heaven—between God and Satan (Job 1:6-12). Here we find that Satan was the one who accused Job, and Satan was also the one who afflicted him. Repeatedly, Satan said to God, "Put forth your hand, and afflict him," but God responded, "He is in your hand" (Job 2:5, 6). The trial which Job underwent was precipitated and administered by Satan.

It was Satan's idea to test Job; he wanted to provoke Job into forsaking and cursing God.

2. The source of sickness—Satan

When calamity befell him, Job, in his ignorance of Satan's activity, said, "The Lord gave and the Lord has taken away', (Job 1:21). Job said this because he was unaware of Satan's activity. Unfortunately, many Christians erroneously quote this very verse in response to the satanic attack of sickness. Job could say this, because he did not have the revelation that is available today under the New Covenant. Christians today have the Word of Jesus declaring, the thief comes only to steal, and kill, and destroy; I came that you might have life, and might have it abundantly"(John 10:10). Keep in mind that the Bible is a progressive revelation of God and His ways. We must interpret the Old Testament in light of the New Testament. God, under this New Covenant, has made it plain to us who the source of sickness and calamity is. In the New Testament, Satan is called the "god of this world" (II Corinthians 4:4). He is the one who causes calamity and destruction in peoples' lives. This is partially revealed in the opening Chapters of the book of Job, although it is not fully elaborated.

3. Our redemption from sickness—Jesus

Thus, today, under this glorious New Covenant, none can claim to be "just like poor old Job." None can say, "The Lord is afflicting me!" or "The

Lord gave, and the Lord has taken away," because God has shown us who the source of calamity is. To say that God will put sickness on us to test us or to purify us is contrary to the work of the cross. God will not place on His children what it cost the life Of His Son to redeem us from the idea that God places sickness on us is incompatible with the fact that God made healing a part of the atoning work of Jesus. The scriptures speak for themselves concerning sickness and disease. "He Himself took our infirmities, and carried away our diseases" (Matthew 8:17). "He Himself bore our sins in His body on the cross that we might die to sin and live to righteousness; for by His wounds you were healed" (I Peter 2:24).

B. PAUL'S THORN

Many are of the opinion that God sometimes says "No!" in answer to prayers for healing. This is often held forth as the reason why some don't receive healing when prayed for. It is thought that sickness is God's method of humbling us, and bringing us closer to Himself. The basis for this type of thinking is an erroneous concept of Paul's thorn in the flesh. Paul speaks of this thorn in his second letter to the Corinthians (II Corinthians 12:7-10).

Here, Paul declares that he received a messenger from Satan (a demon) to buffet him, so that he would not be puffed up with pride concerning the revelations which he had been given. His twice-repeated prayer for deliverance was met with God's answer, "My grace is sufficient for you, for (My) power is perfected in weakness" (II Corinthians 12:9). The "weakness" to which Paul refers is mistakenly thought to be physical sickness, thus leaving the impression that sickness is God's way of keeping His people humble. Much has been written and said on this theme, to the extent that it is now a prevalent idea in the Body of Christ.

1. Persecution
Equating Paul's thorn in the flesh with disease is an assumption which the scriptures do not bear out. Paul enumerates just exactly what his "weakness" entailed. "Therefore I am well content with weaknesses, with insults, with distresses, with persecutions, with difficulties, for Christ's sake" (II Corinthians 12:10). In three other places within his epistles, Paul lists the difficulties which he faced as a result of his preaching the gospel. (Read I Corinthians 4:11-13; II Corinthians 6:4-5;

II Corinthians 11:23-26.) In these references, Paul lists many troubles which he experienced as a servant of Christ, such as persecution, hunger, danger, etc. And yet nowhere, in any of these lists, does Paul ever mention sickness or disease.

The weaknesses which Paul speaks of are the persecutions and trials he encountered at the hands of men because he was preaching the Gospel. In the Old Testament, God told the children of Israel that the Canaanites would become "thorns in the side," if they didn't utterly destroy them from off the land (Numbers 33:55; Joshua 23:13). The "thorns" to which God is referring were people, the Canaanites. In the same way, Paul suffered greatly at the hands of Jews who stirred up trouble for him wherever he went (Acts 13:45,50; 14:2,19; 17:5,13; 18:12; 21:27; 23:12). Paul suffered much from these "thorns" because he preached the Gospel, and it was this from which he sought to be delivered, not from a physical sickness.

God's response to Paul, "My grace is sufficient," is often misunderstood to mean that we are to "bear up" under sickness by the grace of God. But, we are not to "bear up" under anything from which God has redeemed us. God has not redeemed us from persecution (II Timothy 3:12), but He has redeemed us from all disease and illness. God's grace is sufficient to see us through persecution, but the stripes of Jesus are sufficient to take away all sickness from our bodies!

2. Suffering for Jesus?

It is obvious to see from the above that those who are bound with disease are not "suffering for Jesus' sake." Paul's lists of troubles for the sake of the Gospel are explicit, and sickness is conspicuous in its absence from these lists. Suffering for Christ's sake refers strictly to those trials which arise because a person is a believer and preaches the Gospel. Paul could have eliminated all those problems by simply returning to his home town, and malting tents! Being sick is not in any way, shape or form "suffering for Christ's sake"! If that were so, then only Christians would be sick, since only Christians will be persecuted for Christ's sake. However, anybody can be sick, Christian and non—Christian alike. Sickness was not a part of Paul's "troubles" for the sake of the Gospel. The same is true today. If a believer is sick or physically infirm, he is not suffering for Jesus' sake. He is being oppressed by the devil.

Sickness is not the will of God; it is a work of Satan which came about as the result of man's fall. This fact must remain uppermost in a believer's mind if he wants to receive healing or remain healthy. The enemy for centuries has perpetrated the lie God wants His obedient servants and children to be bound up with illness and disease, and unfortunately the Church at large has accepted that judgment.

But, the Bible declares that sickness is a curse, an enemy, and an attack from the enemy. Nowhere in the Old or New Testaments is sickness viewed as a blessing. It is always seen as something from which God wants to deliver man. So much is this so, that God placed physical healing within the mighty provision of the atoning work of Jesus. This alone in the scripture stands out as a statement of God's will, God's will is healing, and He proved that by laying on His Son all our sickness and disease.

Anyone who is suffering with disease can know that it is not God's will that he be so; neither is God the one afflicting him. Sickness is the work of Satan, an attack from without to kill, steal and destroy. With this in mind, we can move on to appropriate the divine health that God has provided, knowing that God is for us and not against us.

LESSON ELEVEN

DAY ONE

HEALING—THE WILL OF GOD STUDY QUESTIONS

1. What do the Hebrew and Greek words for salvation imply?

_____

_____

_____

_____

2. List the seven redemptive names of God and what they reveal about Him. (Include the scriptures where these are found)

a. _____

b. _____

c. _____

d. _____

e. _____

f. _____

g. _____

3. Explain why Jesus' healing ministry was much more than just confirmation of His call. How did He prove this?

_____

_____

_____

4. Jesus' ministry consisted of "doing good, healing all who were oppressed by the devil." What does this tell you about the Father who sent Jesus? Why do Jesus' actions prove it? (Give scripture.)

_____

_____

_____

5. Jesus was the _____ in action on the earth!

259

LESSON ELEVEN HEALING—THE WILL OF GOD
DAY TWO STUDY QUESTIONS

1. How did Jesus view sickness?

   _____

   _____

2. What do Luke 13:16 and Acts 10:38 show us about sickness? How
   does this affect the way in which you view sickness and the manner
   in which you respond to it?

   _____

   _____

3. How do we know that God's healing power and God's willingness
   to heal did not ascend to heaven with Jesus? (Give at least three
   proofs from the scriptures for your answer.)

   _____

   _____

   _____

   How do you know that the Jehovah-Rapha of the Old Testament is
   still Jehovah-Rapha today?

   _____

   _____

   _____

4. God made physical healing a part of the provision of Christ's
   atoning work. Why is this such a profound statement about God's
   will concerning healing?

   _____

   _____

   _____

   _____

LESSON ELEVEN

DAY THREE

HEALING—THE WILL OF GOD, STUDY QUESTIONS

1. What was the Year of Jubilee? What was the significance of the trumpet blast, and what does it signify to us?

_____

_____

_____

2. Why is Isaiah 53 known as the "Great Atonement Chapter"?

_____

_____

_____

What does this chapter tell us about healing and the cross? What New Testament passage proves this connection?

_____

_____

_____

3. How would you respond to a person who felt that sickness was his "cross" to bear? What scriptures would you show him, and how would you explain them?

_____

_____

_____

_____

4. Is it God's will for you to be healed? Explain why you are convinced of this.

_____

_____

_____

LESSON ELEVEN
DAY FOUR
HEALING—THE WILL OF GOD, STUDY QUESTIONS

1. What do you (under the New Covenant) know about sickness and calamity that Job did not know? (Give scripture.)

    _____

    _____

    _____

    How does this affect your interpretation of some of Job's statements? Can you say the same things that he did? Explain.

    _____

    _____

    _____

2. What are the "weaknesses" to which Paul refers in connection with his thorn in the flesh?

    _____

    _____

    _____

    How is this suffering for "Christ's sake" distinct from sickness?

    _____

    _____

    _____

3. In lessons 8, 9 and 10, we learned about faith in God's promises and provisions. In light of what you have learned in those lessons and in this lesson, how would you respond to an attack of sickness in your body? What is your reaction to seeing contradiction of God's Word on healing?

    _____

    _____

Lesson TWELVE DIVINE HEALTH: THE PROVISION OF GOD

Lesson TWELVE DIVINE HEALTH: THE PROVISION OF GOD

I. INTRODUCTION 267

II. HOW TO RECEIVE DIVINE HEALING.................................267
   A. PRAYER 268
      1. The prayer of agreement
      2. The prayer of faith in Jesus' Name
   B. LAYING ON of HANDS 269
      1. The Old Covenant practice
      2. The New Covenant practice
   C. Anointing with Oil..270
   D. The Gifts of Healings...271
      1. As the Spirit wills
      2. Know the difference
   E. The Word and the Name 273
   F. Medicine And Doctors 274
      1. No condemnation
      2. Natural and supernatural assistance

III. HINDRANCES TO RECEIVING HEALING 275
   A. Ignorance..275
   B. Doubt and Unbelief 276
      1. Community unbelief
      2. Individual unbelief
      3. Fear: the reason for wavering
   C. Sin...278
      1. Unforgiveness
      2. Immorality

IV. WALKING IN DIVINE HEALTH..279
   A. Diligence in the Word 280
   B. Obeying Natural Laws..281

V. SUMMARY—THE PATH TO DIVINE HEALTH.....................281

Lesson TWELVE DIVINE HEALTH: THE PROVISION OF GOD

I. INTRODUCTION

Through the redemption purchased by Jesus Christ on Calvary, God has made provision for every believer to walk in divine health. It has never been God's will for His people to be bound and oppressed with sickness and disease. He told the children of Israel that they could have supernatural freedom from illness if they would walk uprightly before Him (Deuteronomy 7:14, 15). God has extended the same promise and provision toward us in the New Covenant, basing it securely in our blood-bought redemption.

Every Christian has the Covenant right to live out his life on this earth free from sickness and disease. Although this does not mean that we will never die death is the last enemy to be conquered by Christ (I Corinthians 15:25, 26), it does mean that we can live free from sickness while in this mortal body. Unfortunately, many Christians today suffer torment at the hands of disease, not availing themselves of the divine health that rightfully belongs to them. But this doesn't change the reality of what He has done. Salvation and forgiveness have been purchased for all men and are offered to all. Yet many, whether through ignorance or unbelief or rebellion, do not receive the forgiveness which is so freely offered to them. The same is true of healing.

God's desire is that His people walk completely free from illness. He purchased our healing on the cross and gave us numerous ways in which we can receive that healing. If we will walk uprightly before Him, and not allow any hindrances to healing into our lives then we will walk in the perfect health which has been made available to us.

II. HOW TO RECEIVE DIVINE HEALING

God is as eager to see the sick healed as the sick are to be released from their ailments and so He has given us numerous methods whereby we can receive the healing which He has purchased for us. Throughout the Old and New Testaments, God has shown us various ways through which His healing power can be appropriated.

Since faith is the means by which anything is received from God, it is not surprising to find that each of these methods requires some degree of faith in order to be effective. "He who comes to God must believe that He is, and that He is a rewarder of those who seek Him." (Hebrews 11:6). Because not every believer's faith is on the same level, God has made these various ways of receiving, healing available to us. God will meet us wherever we are in faith, so that we may always receive, healing from Him.

A. PRAYER

This is perhaps the most obvious method of receiving healing, it is the response of someone in need to seek God in prayer and ask for deliverance. God responds to the prayer of faith offered up by His children and will Move in their behalf when asked by them.

Jesus, specified two basic forms of petition with which we could approach the Father to receive from His hand they are: **1**.) the prayer of agreement, and **2**.) the prayer of **faith** offered in Jesus' Name.

1. The prayer of agreement
Jesus, said, "Again I say to you, that if two of you agree on earth about **anything** that they may ask, it shall be done for them by My Father who is in heaven" (Matthew 18:19). Jesus' promise was that any need, will be met, including that of healing, if; two or more believers will stand together in faith as to the outcome of their prayer. God the Father will do whatever they had agreed upon. The central issue in this method is that of "agreement." **All parties involved must be of one mind as to God's will in the matter and as to their faith in the final outcome.** If the person seeking healing is prayed for and yet he himself still believes his illness to be the will of God, then the prayer of agreement will be ineffective. Before praying the prayer of agreement, it is wise to first determine if everyone involved is indeed in agreement.

2. The prayer of faith in Jesus' Name
Jesus also told His disciples, "I tell you the truth, My Father will give you whatever you ask **in my name.** Until now you have not asked for anything in my name. Ask and you will receive, and your joy will be complete" (John 16:23, 24). Again, Jesus says that anything that we ask for will be

granted, and this includes physical healing. The prayer of faith made in Jesus' Name will bring results to those who are in need.

The Gospels do not specifically record prayer for the sick in the healing ministry of Jesus and His disciples. (The more common methods were lying on of hands and speaking the Word.) However, elsewhere in the New Testament, we do find instances of prayer for the sick. Paul prayed for the father of Publius on the island of Melita (Acts 28:8). The apostle James specifically instructs that those who are sick are to be prayed for in the Name of the Lord (James 5:15, 16). "Therefore confess your sins to one another, and pray for one another, so that you may be healed" (James 5:16). It is obvious that prayer for the sick was a common practice in the first century church.

The promise of Jesus still holds today. Those that ask the Father in Jesus' Name, and believe, will receive from the Father's hand the things that they need from Him. If that need is healing, then the prayer of faith in Jesus' Name will bring about a cure for the one who is sick.

B. LAYING ON OF HANDS

The laying on of hands is by far the most commonly recorded method by which Jesus ministered healing to those who were sick. Although He sometimes simply spoke words over those who were ill (Matthew 8:7, 8, 13; 9:6, 7), most of the time He laid His hands on the sick to heal them (Matthew 8:14, 15; Mark 1:40; 7:32-35; Luke 4:40; 5:12, 13). Jesus said, just prior to His ascension that this practice would continue among His followers. "They will lay hands on the sick, and they will recover" (Mark 16:18). It is apparent from the book of Acts that, this is what happened (Acts 5:12; 19:11); lying on of hands is also listed as one of the foundational doctrines of the Church (Hebrews 6:1, 2).

1. The Old Covenant practice

The laying on of hands is a practice that goes back to the Old Covenant. Under the Old Covenant, it was done in order to transfer inheritance and authority to children or successors. Jacob laid his hands on his grandchildren, Ephraim and Manasseh, to pronounce a blessing over each of them (Genesis 48:14-16). Moses laid his hands on Joshua to transfer his authority and ruler ship over to him (Numbers 27:18). Lying on of hands was also used to impute the sin of Israel to the scapegoat (Leviticus 16:21). In each of these instances, lying on of hands involved a transfer of something from one party to another.

2. The New Covenant practice

When Jesus came into physical contact with those who had need of healing, there flowed from His person power to bring about healing in their bodies. Part of their body that was ailing (Matthew 9:29; 20:34; Mark 7:33) the principle that emerges from this is that the power which Jesus had was transferable to the bodies of the sick by physical contact. Hence, we find that the crowds asked Jesus if they could just touch the hem of His cloak to receive that healing power into their bodies; those who touched Him were made whole (Matthew 14:35,36; Mark 6:56). "And the entire multitude was trying to touch Him, for power was coming from Him and healing them all"(Luke6:19).

When Jesus laid-hands on the Sick, He didn't do it for ceremonial reasons the laying on of hands is not a "symbolic" ritual. It is a means by which the power and Anointing of God can be transferred to the sick. In the town of Capernaum, the entire-city brought their sick, and Jesus laid His hands on every one of them to heal them (Luke 4:40). The power of God was transferred from Jesus to those sick bodies when Jesus touched them, or when they touched—even a part of His clothing. The Acts Of the Apostles records that this healing anointing was even retained in cloth, so that pieces of Paul's clothing 'could be taken to the sick, and the power of God which remained in the cloth was enough to effect release for those afflicted (Acts 19:11,12).

Today, this is still a God-given way for receiving healing. Jesus said that believers would lay their hands on the sick, and they would recover. Because the life and power of God resides within every believer, every believer has the ability to transfer that life and power to a person who is in need of healing. Lying on of hands is still one of God's ways of transmitting His healing power into the bodies of the sick.

C. ANOINTING WITH OIL

Anointing with oil also has its roots in the Old Covenant. In that dispensation, people and things were consecrated to God by anointing them with oil. The Tabernacle and its furniture, built by Moses, were dedicated for service in this way (Exodus 30:25, 26). Prophets (I Kings 19:16), priests (Exodus 28:41), and kings (I Samuel 9:16; 10:1; I Samuel 16:1, 12, 13) were set apart and endued for service by being anointed with oil.

It was symbolic of the Holy Spirit, which came upon these men to empower them for service. The oil was a visual reminder that they were covered by the Holy Spirit (Psalm 133:2).

In the New Testament, the sacred practice of anointing with oil is found in connection with the healing of the sick. When the disciples were sent out by Jesus to preach and heal the sick, the Bible records that they anointed the sick with oil and healed them (Mark 6:12, 13). This was not a medicinal anointing, such as was common in that day (Luke 10:34); it was a sacred, symbolic anointing which resulted in supernatural healing. Thus, James commands that the elder's pray for the sick, " . . . Anointing him with oil in the name of the Lord" (James 5:14).

James makes it clear that it is the prayer of faith which saves the sick (James 5:15). Oil cannot supernaturally heal anyone. But the oil does give the one who is ill a point of contact for his faith. His faith is not in the oil, but in God; the oil helps him to engage his faith toward the fact that the power of God is going into his body to effect a cure in him. The oil is symbolic of the presence of the Holy Spirit, coming upon that person to drive out disease.

D. THE GIFTS OF HEALINGS

In his first letter to the Corinthians, Paul lists nine spiritual gifts; among these nine gifts that are enumerated is "the gifts of healing" (I Corinthians 12:9) the original Greek makes both words plural, yielding gifts of healings). Kenneth Hagin defames the gifts of healings in the following way: "It is a supernatural manifestation of healing power through one individual to another." Each of the nine gifts, including the gifts of healings, is given for "the common good" (I Corinthians 12:7) the Gifts of healings then is another distinct method by which people can obtain healing from the Lord.

"And God has appointed in the church, first apostles, second prophets, third teachers, then miracles, then gifts of healings, helps, administrations;

various kinds of tongues" (I Corinthians 12:28). God has appointed men who are supernaturally gifted in the areas listed. Thus, gifts of healings refers not to a person receiving healing from the Lord (even though all healing comes from Him, whether directly or indirectly), but rather it refers to God supernaturally empowering men in the body of Christ to bring about cures in people's bodies. Sometimes God anoints men for healing of particular areas of the body (e.g. ears, eyes, or backs); that is why this spiritual gift is plural, "gifts of healings." This is not merely a generalized power to heal. It is a specific anointing for a specific need at a specific time.

1. As the Spirit wills

The operations of the gifts of healings (as with any of the other spiritual gifts) are manifested as the Spirit wills, and not as man wills (I Corinthians 12:11). In other words, men cannot dictate how and when the gifts of healings are going to operate; that is entirely up to God. Very often, the person who receives healing as a result of this gift has operated little faith or no faith at all; God has sovereignly moved in their behalf. This was evident with the widow of Nain's dead son (Luke 7:11-17). When Jesus raised him from the dead, the mother wasn't exercising any faith, and the dead son certainly was not. Yet the gifts of healings operated through Jesus, and the dead man was raised. This was a special anointing from the Holy Spirit to bring about the resurrection of a dead man.

2. Know the difference

That the gifts of healings operate only as the Spirit wills means that we can't always explain why some do not receive healing in this way. It is important that we understand the difference between these types of healings, which are initiated sovereignly by God, and those which are initiated by the faith of a believer. God sometimes sovereignly moves to heal as He did at the pool of Bethesda (John 5:2-4). But when God is moving in this manner, not all receive their healing in this particular way. This is not to say that others could not be healed by exercising their faith. Often, those who witness the gifts of healings in operation are stirred to exercise their own faith and receive their healing from the Lord.

However, no sick person can dictate to God that the healings must operate in their behalf. Only the Spirit can dictate how and when this spiritual gift will operate. Thus, it is foolish to wait for God to move sovereignly in one's own behalf, when God has made many other ways of receiving healing available to us. Not everyone will be healed by the sovereign move of God, apart from their own faith. But, all those who exercise faith in God's Word and obey the instructions for receiving healing that He has given there can receive from God, without having to wait upon a sovereign action of God—which may never come.

E. THE WORD AND THE NAME

As we have seen, the Word of God is explicit as to what belongs to us through the redemptive work of Jesus. When attacked by physical symptoms of sickness, we can simply stand on the Word of God and confess the truth of that Word which declares, "By His wounds you were healed" (1 Peter 2:24). Jesus Christ bore all sickness and pain; so that we would not have to suffer with it The Bible clearly states that healing is part of the Redemptive plan of God for our lives. This means that we must have an understanding of our healing being a past-tense reality, rather than a future-tense expectation.

This does not mean that it is wrong' or in any way displeasing to God if we receive healing by any of the other methods which we have listed. God Himself is the One who instituted the methods-which we' have enumerated. But, God desires that His children reach a level of faith and scriptural understanding from which they can resist the devil when he attacks with sickness, and defeat him. Thus, He has given us His Word and the Name of Jesus to combat the forces of Satan and defeat them.

When Peter met the lame man at the Beautiful gate, he commanded him to be healed in Jesus Name. He later told the on looking crowd that it was Jesus Name and faith in that Name which had healed the man (Acts 3:16). We have been given the Word of God, which informs us of our covenant rights. And we have been given the Name of Jesus which is above every name (Philippians 2:9). With these two weapons every: believer should be able to resist the devil when he attacks with illness. This is, the best way to receive healing from the Lord, because once one has stood on the Word for healing and received, it is not as likely that he will have that healing stolen from him, as so often happens to those who receive by a sovereign move Of God. The one who has stood on the Word knows how to deal with the lying symptoms of the enemy.

F. MEDICINE AND DOCTORS

A commonly, asked question concerning divine healing regards the place of medical science The primary thing one must recognize about physicians and medical science is that they view sickness and disease in the same way as God does; it is an enemy which they seek to eradicate. Medical science and divine healing are not antithetical. Doctors are fighting the same foe that God, through divine healing, opposes.

1. No condemnation

A Christian should never feel condemned if he ever uses the services of a physician. It is not necessarily "unbelief" to use medicine, just as it is not necessarily "faith" to stop using medicine. Many have stopped using prescribed medication, thinking that this outward action, in and of itself, was faith, and many have suffered needlessly because of their misunderstanding. Faith is of the heart, it is an inward rest and assurance, not merely an outward action. Thus, a person can build his faith for complete deliverance while still on medication for an illness. Faith and medicine are not enemies; they are allies.

2. Natural and supernatural assistance

One must make a distinction between the methods used by God and by medicine. Medicine uses natural means to eliminate disease; divine healing is God using supernatural means to do so. These two must not be confused. Doubtless, God is indirectly behind the great medical advances made in the recent past, since many lives have been saved and many people helped.

But, healing by medical science and healing by God are not the same. One is natural, while the other is completely supernatural. God's perfect will is that none of His children ever experience sickness. If we are attacked by the enemy in this area, then God wants us to be healed. If a person's faith isn't to a point where healing is being manifested, then God isn't opposed to that person seeking whatever help medical science can give. But, God wants us to grow in faith. Believers should always be striving to develop their faith and patience to a point where they don't need natural assistance, but can stand on the Word and receive supernatural healing from the Lord. This is God's best way of receiving healing, even though He doesn't condemn or upbraid those that seek such help as medical science can offer.

III. HINDRANCES TO RECEIVING HEALING

Whenever one discusses divine healing, the questions often arise: "What about those who fail to receive divine healing? Did God fail them? Did He fail to perform what He said in His Word?" Of course, we know that God cannot fail. He is utterly faithful and true. Thus, when healing does not come, we cannot look to God, as if the fault for this failure lay with Him. Those who do not receive healing cannot say to God, "You have failed to do what Your Word says you will do!"

Since God cannot lie and He cannot fail His Word, then the responsibility for failure to receive healing must lie with us, and not with God. When a person is not healed, many times it's due to some hindrance in that person's life, which is blocking the power of God from flowing into his body.

When these hindrances are dealt with and removed, then healing will come. God is always willing to heal, but sometimes actions or attitudes within those seeking healing hinder God from being able to perform His Word in their behalf.

A. IGNORANCE

Very often, people fail to receive healing simply because they are ignorant of the fact that healing has been provided in our redemption. They don't know that by His wounds we were healed, nor do they know that Jesus Himself bore our infirmities. They aren't even aware that it is God's will for them to be well. In the last lesson, we saw that knowledge of God's will is necessary before one can appropriate what God has freely given to us. "Faith comes by hearing, and hearing by the Word of God" (Romans 10:17). This is as true of healing as it is of salvation. Faith for healing comes as one hears the Word of God which declares God's will and His provision in the matter.

Thus, as long as a person remains ignorant of the Word's declaration about freedom from sickness, he will be hindered from receiving healing. He will never be sure that it is really God's will to heal, because he hasn't yet heard the "good news" concerning healing. But when a person begins to meditate in God's Word and dispels his ignorance with spiritual understanding, then faith will arise within his heart, and he will be able to receive the healing that he is seeking.

Many Christians, in their ignorance of God's Word and will, have prayed for healing using the phrase, "If it be Thy will!" They believe that God's answer will be evident by how the circumstances work out. And if healing does not come, they place themselves in a category with Job, saying, "The Lord gave, and the Lord has taken away" (Job 1:21). The hindrance of ignorance has kept many from receiving healing from the Lord.

B. DOUBT AND UNBELIEF

Another great hindrance to receiving healing is doubt and unbelief. Doubt and unbelief will keep a person from receiving from the Lord, because they hinder the hand of God from moving. Jesus often reprimanded His disciples for the littleness of their faith, and He rebuked those who simply did not believe in the power of God that was operating through Him.

Unbelief can arise in two forms: corporate or community unbelief and individual unbelief. Both are equally effective in their power to hinder one from being healed by the power of God.

1. Community unbelief

Jesus called the generation among which He walked an "unbelieving and perverted generation" (Matthew 17:17). These words Jesus addressed not to His disciples, but to the crowd that had surrounded them after their failure to deliver a demon-possessed boy (Luke 9:37-43). Jesus was aware of the unbelief prevalent among the whole mass of those people.

This same kind of community unbelief hindered Jesus from doing any great miracles in His own home town of Nazareth (Mark 6:5, 6; Matthew 13:57, 58). These scriptures do not indicate that Jesus was unwilling to perform any miracles in Nazareth; His compassion for the people of Nazareth was no less than for the people of any other town. But the Bible says, "He could do no miracle there" (i.e. He was not able) (Mark 6:5), and affirms that the hindrance was their corporate unbelief (Matthew 13:58).

Community unbelief often manifests itself in the form of religious traditions. This is evident in the various erroneous concepts about healing that are prevalent among Christians. The tradition which says that the age of miracles has passed is community unbelief, because it is so widely accepted in the Church. Religious tradition often is ingrained in a person's thinking without that person being consciously aware of it. It is simply a part of the society in which he lives and moves, and thus has become a part of his thinking. But this hindrance can be easily removed by rejecting the traditions of men, and cleaving wholeheartedly to the Word of God.

2. Individual unbelief

When the disciples asked Jesus why they were not able to cast the demon out of a boy, Jesus didn't pamper them with soft answers; He simply told them the truth: "Because of the littleness of your faith" (Matthew 17:20). This often isn't the type of answer people like to hear when faced with a failure to receive healing from the Lord.

But, very often it is the very reason for that failure. Jesus said that if we would speak to the mountain, it would obey us if we did not doubt in our hearts (Mark 11:23). The hindering factor that will keep the mountain from obeying us is doubt, or wavering on God's Word. The apostle James said that the one who wavers should not expect to receive anything from the Lord (James 1:6-8). Doubt or wavering (by which we mean being caught between two opinions) will block the power of God from operating in a person's behalf. Individual unbelief and doubt are overcome in the same way as community unbelief: through diligent meditation in God's Word concerning healing. Only as a person begins to take in the truth of God's Word will he dispel the unbelief.

3. Fear: the reason for wavering

Christians often waver in their conviction concerning the healing power of God because they fear that this time God will not be faithful to His Word. The enemy often uses fear to shake a believer off his conviction of God's faithfulness. When this happens, a person will begin to waver between two opinions: the one—God's Word is true, and God is true to His Word; the other—this time, God is not going to come through. It is a vacillation between faith and fear, hope and despondency.

This type of wavering is often the reason why many don't receive the healing that they are seeking. God is not unwilling to heal, but a person's unbelief hinders His mighty hand, just as the unbelief of Jesus' home town hindered Him from doing any miracles there. The fear that leads to wavering can be countered by meditating upon God's faithfulness. God is faithful to His Word and will not fail to perform it if we will retain our confidence in Him and in His Word. The Bible exhorts us not to cast away our fearless confidence (Hebrews 10:35 Amplified). If we will remove the hindrance of wavering and hold on to our confidence in God and His Word, the promised results will come.

C. SIN

Sometimes sin and disobedience to God are reasons why people don't receive healing from the Lord. The Bible states explicitly that sin will hinder a person's prayers from being answered. "If I regard wickedness in my heart, the Lord will not hear" (Psalm 66:18). "The face of the Lord is against evildoers, to cut off the memory of them from the earth" (Psalm 34:16). If a person is openly practicing sin, he cannot expect to receive healing. The apostle Paul states that the sin of abusing the Lord's Supper caused the sickness and early death of a number of believers in the Corinthian church (I Corinthians 11:28-30). Their wanton abuse of the communion table resulted in sickness.

The solution to the hindrance of sin is simple: repent! To repent means to turn around and stop doing the thing that you are doing. From time to time Christians need to examine themselves to see if there is anything that they are doing which is contrary to the Word and the Law of God (II Corinthians 13:5). This doesn't mean that we assume that there is something wrong; but it does mean that we shouldn't assume that there is not anything wrong. The Bible says that we are to examine ourselves; if we do this honestly, God will show us if there is anything that needs correction, so that we can deal with it.

"(If) My people who are called by My name humble themselves and pray, and seek My face and turn from their wicked ways, then I will hear from heaven, will forgive their sin, and will heal their land" (II Chronicles 7:14). This God Spoke to Israel as a people. But, the same principle holds true for every believer individually. If sin is a hindrance to healing, then repentance will turn the situation around, bringing the power of God on the scene with healing.

1. Unforgiveness
"And whenever you stand praying, forgive, if you have anything against anyone; so that your Father also who is in heaven may forgive you your

transgressions" (Mark 11:25). We live in an imperfect world, where people tread on our toes and wrong us, knowingly and unknowingly. Thus, for the believer, forgiveness must become a way of life. However, when a Christian harbors bitterness in his heart against another, this often hinders God from moving in his behalf for healing. This scripture makes it plain that unforgiveness blocks God from moving in any way on our behalf; those who will not forgive are not walking uprightly before God. God has forgiven us such a massive debt; we have no right to withhold forgiveness from anyone, no matter what may have been done to us. One cannot expect God to heal him if he is knowingly bearing a grudge against another (i.e. knowingly sinning!).

2. Immorality

It should go without saying that anyone who engages in such practices as fornication (i.e. sex outside of marriage), adultery, theft, lying, etc. cannot with good conscience stand in faith for healing. Yet many times, blatant sin like this is overlooked by some, while they simultaneously seek healing from the Lord. The Bible says that God's ears are open to the prayer of those who walk uprightly, whose hearts are right towards Him. But a person who blatantly sins, knowing that it is wrong, will not be heard by God (I Peter 3:12). Although that healing is not a "reward" for clean living, openly living in sin will be a hindrance to anyone who desires to be healed by the power of God.

IV. WALKING IN DIVINE HEALTH

God's best for His children is that they live totally free from illness. This is a state of divine health. Divine healing is the provision that God has made for those who are experiencing sickness. But His best is that we live completely free from the oppression of sickness, walking by faith and defeat the enemy every time he tries to afflict us with symptoms of disease.

This does not mean that we should be condemned if we are attacked by the devil; it is simply a statement of God's perfect will for His people. The adversary may well attack, but a believer with a firm knowledge of the Word and the will of God will resist that onslaught and win.

In order to live in divine health, there are certain things which the believer must do. No one will ever receive anything from the Lord without exercising some degree of diligence. Laziness is not the way to receive from the Lord. There are also certain natural laws which cannot be ignored if one is to remain in health. God will not bless or condone stupidity. But if a believer will obey the Word of God and fulfill the criteria which the Word lays out, then he can expect to be able to live in divine health, successfully thwarting the attempts of the enemy to place sickness on him.

A. DILIGENCE IN THE WORD

Faith for healing and health, as faith for anything else, comes from diligent meditation in the Word of God. The Bible says that God is a rewarder of those who "earnestly" seek Him (Hebrews 11:6). When we seek the Lord or the things of the Lord, we must do so with all our hearts. "And you will seek me and find me, when you search for me with all your heart". (Jeremiah 29:13) No one will receive from the Lord with a half-hearted attitude toward God, and His Word. The Bible declares that the Word of God is health to a person's flesh, if he will be diligent with it. "My son give attention to my words; incline your ear to My sayings. Do not let them depart from your sight; keep them in the midst of your heart. For they are life to those who find them, and health to all their flesh" (Proverbs 4:20-22) this is God's "prescription" for divine health. We must give the same kind of diligence to God's "prescription" for healing and health, as we would give to a doctor's prescription for better health. The expressions "give attention," and "incline your ear" indicate wholehearted attention to the Word of God. When this wholehearted attention is given to the Word, then the Word will become health (or "medicine" KJV marginal reading) to a person's flesh. If God's prescription is taken as directed, then the promised results will be manifested in a believer's life.

B. OBEYING NATURAL LAWS

While we live in our mortal bodies, we are still subject to the laws of nature which govern it. Divine healing through the Word and the power of God is not a license for presumption. Thus, while one can believe God for healing from the attack of disease, one cannot believe God for health while simultaneously abusing his body. Divine healing goes only so far as the Bible promises. The Word says that we can be healed of all disease (Psalm 103:3) and live free of its oppression (Exodus 23:25, 26). But, nowhere does the Bible promise us we can be reckless and irresponsible with our bodies and expect to stay well.

Unwisely driving our bodies beyond their point of endurance will result in sickness, because God will not bless or endorse foolishness. Believers have a responsibility to take proper care of their own temples; from this stance they can stand against Satan's attacks of illness. For example, it would be presumption for a Christian to go without sleep for days at a time, while all the time believing God to remain in perfect health. It would be foolish for a Christian to stop eating altogether, and then believe God that he could survive with no food. The Bible does not promise that we will never tire physically, nor does it promise that we can live without food. It simply promises that we can live out our lives in these mortal bodies free from sickness and disease.

We are accountable to take proper care of our bodies, for they are the temples of the Holy Spirit (I Corinthians 6:19). When we act sensibly, and not foolishly, then we can expect the blessing of divine health. But if we abuse our bodies, ignoring the laws of nature, then we must repent. Foolishness and presumption will hinder a believer from walking in the divine health that God has for every one of His children.

V. SUMMARY—THE PATH TO DIVINE HEALTH

Divine health (that state of being in which one is not always seeking healing, but rather is enjoying health and successfully countering the attacks of the enemy) is God's provision for the entire body of Christ. That many in the Church don't experience this does not change the fact that it is God's will. Through His Word, God has revealed to us numerous ways by which we can be freed from sickness and begin to walk in divine health. The prayer of agreement, the prayer of faith in Jesus' Name, laying on of hands and anointing . . . with oil (to name a few), were all given by God so that the sick could receive deliverance from illness.

But by far the best way for a believer to be healed is simply to claim his covenant right by faith and confess the Word concerning his healing. This is the path of growth, a path which leads to a place where the attacks of the devil are more and more easily thwarted. A believer who has successfully stood on the Word for his healing is not ignorant of any of Satan's devices and knows how to deal with them better when they arise again. Until the Lord Jesus returns, no believer will ever get to a place where the enemy cannot attack him. But a Christian can grow to a place where Satan's attacks are easier and easier to deal with through the Word.

LESSON TWELVE

DAY ONE

DIVINE HEALTH—THE PROVISION OF GOD STUDY QUESTIONS

1. There are a number of different ways of receiving healing. What requirement is common to all of them?

   _____

2. Some mistakenly equate the idea of divine health with the idea that this mortal body is not subject to death. What is the distinction between these two ideas?

   _____

   _____

   _____

   _____

3. What are two types of prayer that Jesus taught, that can be used to receive healing from God? Briefly explain each. (Give scriptures.)

   a. _____

   b. _____

4. Why did Jesus lay His hands on the sick, and what was occurring when He did? What does this show us about the healing anointing of God?

   _____

   _____

   _____

   _____

LESSON TWELVE

DAY TWO

DIVINE HEALTH—THE PROVISION OF GOD STUDY QUESTIONS

1. When a person is anointed with oil, what does the oil symbolize?

   _____

2. Oil itself does not heal. What, then, is the purpose behind the oil?

   _____

   _____

3. Briefly, what are gifts of healings? How do they operate? Who determines when and where the gifts of healings will operate?

   _____

   _____

   _____

4. "I know God heals people. I've seen Him touch people at meetings. I'm just waiting for Him to touch me with the hand of healing!" How would you counsel a person who said this? What does this person need to understand?

   _____

   _____

   _____

   _____

5. What is the best method by which we can receive healing? Explain why this is so.

   _____

   _____

   _____

   _____

LESSON TWELVE

DAY THREE

DIVINE HEALTH—THE PROVISION OF GOD STUDY QUESTIONS

1. List the five methods given in this lesson for receiving healing, with a Bible example for each one.

   a. _____

   _____

   b. _____

   _____

   c. _____

   _____

   d. _____

   _____

   e. _____

   _____

2. In what ways are divine healing and medical science alike?

   _____

   In what ways are they distinct from one another?

   _____

   _____

3. Is it always unbelief for a believer to take medicine? Why or why not?

   _____

   _____

   Unbelief can arise in two forms. What are they? Briefly explain what is involved in each. Give an example of each from the scriptures.

   a. _____

   b. _____

LESSON TWELVE
DAY FOUR
DIVINE HEALTH—THE PROVISION OF GOD STUDY QUESTIONS

1. What is the simple solution to the hindrance of sin? What does it entail? (Give scriptures.)

   _____

   _____

   _____

2. What is "divine health?" What is God's prescription for maintaining a life of divine health?

   _____

   _____

   _____

   _____

3. A certain Christian brother abuses his body through neglect and overwork, all the while believing for divine health. Is this person really standing on God's Word? Why or why not?

   _____

   _____

   _____

   _____

   _____

4. How do you make provision for divine health in your own life and the lives of your family?

   _____

   _____

   _____

   _____